Ninja Foodi Digital Air Fry Oven Cookbook

150 Quick, Delicious & Easy-to-Prepare Recipes for Your Family

Lisa Hutchinson

Table of Contents

Introduction

If you are looking for the ultimate kitchen companion that could bake, Air Fry, toast, dehydrate, and broil a variety of food all in one place, then Ninja Foodi Digital Air Fry Oven is the right fit for you. This advance Air Fry oven is not only multipurpose but also saves much space on your kitchen counter due to its smart flip design. Imagine, instead of having a toaster, an Air Fryer, and an oven separately lying on your kitchen shelf, you will have one single appliance which can do all of that with much efficiency. This 8-in-1 multipurpose Ninja oven is extremely user-friendly and gives its users complete control over both the cooking temperature and time. And this Ninja Foodi digital Air Fry oven cookbook is about to bring you all the irresistibly delicious recipes that you can cook in your new Ninja digital Air Fryer oven.

Ninja Foodi Digital Air Fry Oven

The Ninja Digital Air Fry oven has made it possible for every user to cook and enjoy fresh and crispy meals in no time. It is an electric oven that has merged with other smart cooking features like Air Frying, broiling, roasting, toasting, and dehydrating. This appliance is especially good for people who love to bake and cook crispy food. When you buy the 8 in 1 Ninja Air Fry oven SP101, here is what you are going in to get inside the box:

- The Ninja Digital Air Fry oven main unit with the flip design
- An Air Fry basket
- A Roast tray
- A Sheet pan
- A removable crumb tray

Unlike conventional oven or Air Fryers, the Ninja Foodi digital Air Fry oven comes with an adjustable space feature, which means that you can place the oven both horizontally and vertically over the kitchen shelf. For cooking, the oven can be placed in its horizontal position. And when not in use, the cleaned oven can be flipped to stand vertically on the shelf. This creates an extra space over the shelf without doing much. Just make sure to flip the oven only when it is completely cooled and clean.

This Air Fry oven comes with 8 functions in one. A user can Air Fryer, Air Roast, bake, toast bread and bagel, dehydrate and broil food just on a press of a button. You can also switch from one mode to another during the cooking if needed. The toast and bagel function give you options to select the darkness of the bread as desired.

Quick User Guide

If you are completely new to this appliance, then here is how you can cook using its different cooking functions:

1. First, check all the components of the appliance and see if they all intact and in good shape.
2. To use the appliance for the first time, clean or wash its cooking accessories like the baking pan, sheet pan, and Air Fryer basket and let them completely dry.
3. Now plug in the device and press the "Power button" given on the control panel.
4. After pressing this button, the LED will light up and indicate the device is one.
5. Place the crumb tray at the bottom of the oven.
6. The Ninja Foodi digital Air Fry oven quickly preheats itself, so it is recommended to place the food inside and then set the mode, time, and temperature accordingly. Or at least keep the food ready to place inside the oven when it is preheated.
7. Place the prepared food inside and close the lid or door of the Ninja Foodi digital Air Fry oven.
8. To do so, first select the cooking mode. Rotate the dial, and it will switch between the modes. Stop rotating the dial when the blue light appears beside your desired mode.
9. After selecting the function, it's time to change the temperature and time settings.
10. To change the cooking time, first press the "Time" button and then rotate the dial to increase or decrease the number of minutes.
11. Similarly, to change the temperature, press the "Temp" button and rotate the dial to adjust the temperature according.
12. It is to note here that the "Time" button is also used to select the number of "Slices" when the oven is running on the "Toast" and "Bagel" mode, and the "Temp" button is used to set the level of "darkness" of the toasts on the given modes.
13. Initiate Cooking:
14. When the mode, temp, and time are adjusted, the device is ready to use.
15. For Baking, Air Frying, Air Roasting, and Broiling, the device takes some time to preheat.
16. It starts to preheat when the Dial is pressed to start the cooking.
17. At this point, the Led screen will show PRE in red color, and the timer does not start ticking until the PRE sign disappears and the device is preheated.
18. Once it is preheated, the device beeps to indicate that it will now automatically start cooking, and its timer will start running.
19. When the food is cooked, the device keeps it warm until you are ready to remove it from the oven.

Breakfast Recipes

Ham Brie Sandwich

Prep Time: 15 minutes.

Cook Time: 10 minutes.

Serves: 2

Ingredients:

- 2 teaspoons butter salted
- 2 bread slices
- 2 ham slices
- 1 tablespoon blueberry BBQ sauce
- 3 oz. brie cheese, sliced

Preparation:

1. Place the bread slices on the working surface and top them with butter.
2. Add ham and brie slices on top of one bread slice and place the other side on top with its buttered side down.
3. Place this sandwich in the baking tray of the Ninja Foodi Digital Air Fryer oven.
4. Transfer the sandwich to the Ninja Foodi Digital Air Fryer Oven and close the door.
5. Select "Air Crisp" mode by rotating the dial.
6. Press the TEMP button and change the value to 375 degrees F.
7. Press the TIME button and change the value to 10 minutes, then press START to begin cooking.
8. Flip the sandwich after 5 minutes.
9. Slice and serve warm.

Serving Suggestion: Serve the cheese sandwiches with crispy bacon on the side.

Variation Tip: Add a layer of garlic mayonnaise to the sandwich before cooking.

Nutritional Information Per Serving:

Calories 284 | Fat 7.9g |Sodium 704mg | Carbs 46g | Fiber 3.6g | Sugar 6g | Protein 18g

Breakfast Hash

Prep Time: 15 minutes.

Cook Time: 20 minutes.

Serves: 4

Ingredients:

- 1/4 cup unsalted butter, melted
- 1 teaspoon paprika
- 1 ¾ cups russet potatoes, peeled and chopped
- 3/4 cup cooked kielbasa, chopped
- 1 small yellow onion, peeled, chopped
- 1 teaspoon salt

Preparation:

1. Toss potatoes, kielbasa, and onion in a large bowl.
2. Whisk melted butter, salt, and paprika in a small bowl.
3. Pour this mixture over the veggies and toss well to coat.
4. Spread the veggies in the Ninja sheet pan.
5. Transfer the sheet pan to the Ninja Foodi Digital Air Fryer Oven and close the door.
6. Select the "Bake" mode by rotating the dial.
7. Press the TEMP button and change the value to 400 degrees F.
8. Press the TIME button and change the value to 20 minutes, then press START to begin cooking.
9. Toss the veggies once cooked halfway through.
10. Serve warm.

Serving Suggestion: Serve the breakfast hash with crumbled crispy bacon on top and warm bread on the side

Variation Tip: Add chopped carrots and broccoli to the hash.

Nutritional Information Per Serving:

Calories 214 | Fat 5.1g |Sodium 231mg | Carbs 31g | Fiber 5g | Sugar 2.1g | Protein 17g

Breakfast Frittata

Prep Time: 15 minutes.

Cook Time: 12 minutes.

Serves: 4

Ingredients:

- ¼ lb. breakfast sausage, cooked and crumbled
- 4 eggs, beaten
- ½ cup Cheddar-Monterey Jack cheese, shredded
- 2 tablespoons red bell pepper, diced
- 1 green onion, chopped
- 1 pinch cayenne pepper
- Cooking spray

Preparation:

1. Beat eggs in a bowl and stir in cayenne, bell pepper, onion, and cheese.
2. Mix well and pour the egg-mixture into 6x2 inches baking pan.
3. Transfer the baking pan to the Ninja Foodi Digital Air Fryer Oven and close the door.
4. Select the "Bake" mode by rotating the dial.
5. Press the TEMP button and change the value to 400 degrees F.
6. Press the TIME button and change the value to 12 minutes, then press START to begin cooking.
7. Slice and serve warm.

Serving Suggestion: Serve the frittata with toasted French bread slices

Variation Tip: Sausage can be replaced with chopped ham slices.

Nutritional Information Per Serving:

Calories 387 | Fat 6g |Sodium 154mg | Carbs 37.4g | Fiber 2.9g | Sugar 15g | Protein 15g

Chile-Cheese Frittata

Prep Time: 15 minutes.

Cook Time: 12 minutes.

Serves: 4

Ingredients:

- Cooking spray
- 4 eggs
- 3 tablespoons heavy cream
- 2 bacon slices, cooked and crumbled
- ½ cup Jack cheese, shredded
- ¼ cup green chiles, chopped
- 3 tablespoons tomatoes, diced
- 2 tablespoons onion, chopped
- Salt and black pepper, to taste

Preparation:

1. Whisk eggs with cream, bacon, cheese, green chiles, tomatoes, onion, black pepper, and salt in a bowl.

2. Pour this egg mixture into the Ninja baking pan.

3. Transfer the baking pan to the Ninja Foodi Digital Air Fryer Oven and close the door.

4. Select the "Bake" mode by rotating the dial.

5. Press the TEMP button and change the value to 400 degrees F.

6. Press the TIME button and change the value to 12 minutes, then press START to begin cooking.

Serving Suggestion: Serve this frittata with crispy bread toasts.

Variation Tip: Add crumbled sausage to the egg-batter.

Nutritional Information Per Serving:

Calories 304 | Fat 32g |Sodium 890mg | Carbs 4.3g | Fiber 4g | Sugar 8g | Protein 25g

Hasselback Potatoes

Prep Time: 15 minutes.

Cook Time: 15 minutes.

Serves: 4

Ingredients:

- 4 potatoes
- Olive oil, to rub

Preparation:

1. Scrub the potatoes and cut 1/4inch apart slits in each potato while leaving 3/8 inch from the base.
2. Rub the potatoes with olive oil and place them in the Ninja Sheet pan.
3. Transfer the sheet pan to the Ninja Foodi Digital Air Fryer Oven and close the door.
4. Select "Air Crisp" mode by rotating the dial.
5. Press the TEMP button and change the value to 400 degrees F.
6. Press the TIME button and change the value to 15 minutes, then press START to begin cooking.
7. Serve warm.

Serving Suggestion: Serve the potatoes with cheese and bacon toppings.

Variation Tip: Insert a slice of tomato, cheese, and zucchini into the slits of potatoes before baking.

Nutritional Information Per Serving:

Calories 312 | Fat 25g |Sodium 132mg | Carbs 44g | Fiber 3.9g | Sugar 3g | Protein 18.9g

Morning Bagels

Prep Time: 15 minutes.

Cook Time: 9 minutes.

Serves: 6

Ingredients:

- 1 cup self-rising flour
- 1 cup Greek yogurt
- 1/2 cup cream cheese, whipped
- 2 tablespoons cinnamon and sugar
- Toasted sesame seeds

Preparation:

1. Mix flour with Greek yogurt and cream cheese in a bowl.
2. Divide the dough into 6 equal pieces and roll them into a ball.
3. Roll each of the six dough balls into a rope and shape each into a bagel.
4. Place the bagels in the Ninja Air Fryer basket.
5. Transfer the basket to the Ninja Foodi Digital Air Fryer Oven and close the door.
6. Select "Air Crisp" mode by rotating the dial.
7. Press the TEMP button and change the value to 325 degrees F.
8. Press the TIME button and change the value to 9 minutes, then press START to begin cooking.
9. Flip the bagels once cooked halfway through, then resume cooking.
10. Coat the bagels with cinnamon, sugar, and sesame seeds.
11. Serve.

Serving Suggestion: Serve the bagels with fried eggs and crispy bacon.

Variation Tip: Add chopped pecans or walnuts to the batter.

Nutritional Information Per Serving:

Calories 331 | Fat 2.5g |Sodium 595mg | Carbs 69g | Fiber 12g | Sugar 12g | Protein 8.7g

Egg Avocado Boats

Prep Time: 15 minutes.

Cook Time: 12 minutes.

Serves: 2

Ingredients:

- 1 Avocado
- Salt, to taste
- Black pepper to taste
- Cooking spray
- 2 eggs

Preparation:

1. Slice the avocado in half, remove the pit and scoop a teaspoon of flesh from the center.
2. Crack one egg into each avocado and drizzle black pepper and salt on top.
3. Place the avocado in the Ninja Air Fryer basket and spray them with cooking spray.
4. Transfer the Air Fryer basket to the Ninja Foodi Digital Air Fryer Oven and close the door.
5. Select "Air Crisp" mode by rotating the dial.
6. Press the TEMP button and change the value to 390 degrees F.
7. Press the TIME button and change the value to 12 minutes, then press START to begin cooking.
8. Serve warm.

Serving Suggestion: Serve the avocado cups with crispy bacon on top.

Variation Tip: Top egg with fresh herbs or chopped bell pepper.

Nutritional Information Per Serving:

Calories 297 | Fat 15g |Sodium 202mg | Carbs 58.5g | Fiber 4g | Sugar 1g | Protein 7.3g

Breakfast Bombs

Prep Time: 15 minutes.

Cook Time: 19 minutes.

Serves: 4

Ingredients:

- 3 bacon slices
- 3 large eggs, beaten
- 1 oz. cream cheese, softened
- 1 tablespoon fresh chives. chopped
- 4 oz. whole-wheat pizza dough
- Cooking spray

Preparation:

1. Sauté bacon in a skillet for 10 minutes until crispy. Transfer it to a plate and allow it cool
2. Crumble the bacon in a bowl and crack eggs into the bowl.
3. Stir in chives and cream cheese. Then beat well.
4. Cook the egg-bacon mixture in a greased skillet for 5 minutes to get a scramble.
5. Divide the wheat dough into 4 pieces and spread each into a 5-inch circle.
6. Divide the egg mixture on top of the dough circles.
7. Brush the edges of the dough with water and bring the edges together, then pinch them together.
8. Place the balls in the baking tray, greased with cooking spray with their seam side down.
9. Transfer the baking tray to the Ninja Foodi Digital Air Fryer Oven and close the door.
10. Select "Air Crisp" mode by rotating the dial.
11. Press the TEMP button and change the value to 350 degrees F.
12. Press the TIME button and change the value to 9 minutes, then press START to begin cooking.
13. Flip the balls once cooked halfway through, then resume cooking.
14. Serve warm.

Serving Suggestion: Serve these bombs with your hot sauce or any other tangy sauce you like.

Variation Tip: Add sautéed ground chicken or pork to the egg filling.

Nutritional Information Per Serving:

Calories 305 | Fat 15g |Sodium 548mg | Carbs 26g | Fiber 2g | Sugar 1g | Protein 19g

Snacks and Appetizer Recipes

Corn Dog Bites

Prep Time: 15 minutes.

Cook Time: 10 minutes.

Serves: 6

Ingredients:

- 2 beef hot dogs
- 12 craft sticks or bamboo skewers
- 1/2 cup all-purpose flour
- 2 large eggs, beaten
- 1 ½ cups crushed cornflakes cereal
- Cooking spray
- 8 teaspoons yellow mustard

Preparation:

1. Cut each hot dog into six small pieces and insert a craft stick into each piece.
2. Spread flour in one bowl, beat eggs in another bowl, and spread the cornflakes on a plate.
3. Dredge the hot dogs through the flour, dip each in the egg and then coat with the cornflakes.
4. Place the hot dog sticks in the Ninja baking tray and spray them with cooking spray.
5. Transfer the baking tray to the Ninja Foodi Digital Air Fryer Oven and close the door.
6. Select "Air Crisp" mode by rotating the dial.
7. Press the TEMP button and change the value to 375 degrees F.
8. Press the TIME button and change the value to 10 minutes, then press START to begin cooking.
9. Flip the corn dogs once cooked halfway through, then resume cooking.
10. Serve warm.

Serving Suggestion: Serve the corn dogs with tomato ketchup or cheese dip.

Variation Tip: Skip cornflakes and coat the corn dogs with breadcrumbs.

Nutritional Information Per Serving:

Calories 148 | Fat 22g |Sodium 350mg | Carbs 32.2g | Fiber 0.7g | Sugar 1g | Protein 4.3g

Beet Chips

Prep Time: 15 minutes.

Cook Time: 30 minutes.

Serves: 6

Ingredients:

- 3 red beets, peeled and sliced
- 2 teaspoons canola oil
- 3/4 teaspoon salt
- 1/4 teaspoon black pepper

Preparation:

1. Toss the beets with canola oil, black pepper, and salt in a bowl.
2. Spread the seasoned beet slice in the Ninja Air Fryer basket.
3. Transfer the basket to the Ninja Foodi Digital Air Fryer Oven and close the door.
4. Select "Air Crisp" mode by rotating the dial.
5. Press the TEMP button and change the value to 320 degrees F.
6. Press the TIME button and change the value to 30 minutes, then press START to begin cooking.
7. Toss the beets once cooked halfway through, then resume cooking.
8. Serve.

Serving Suggestion: Serve the chips with white cheese dip.

Variation Tip: Drizzle cinnamon ground on top before baking.

Nutritional Information Per Serving:

Calories 47 | Fat 2g |Sodium 48mg | Carbs 6g | Fiber 2g | Sugar 0g | Protein 1g

Cinnamon Apple Chips

Prep Time: 15 minutes.

Cook Time: 12 minutes.

Serves: 4

Ingredients:

- 1 (8-oz.) apple, sliced
- 1 teaspoon ground cinnamon
- 2 teaspoons canola oil
- Cooking spray
- 1/4 cup Greek yogurt
- 1 tablespoon almond butter
- 1 teaspoon honey

Preparation:

1. Toss apple slices with oil and cinnamon in a baking tray.
2. Spread the apple slices in the Ninja Air Fryer basket.
3. Transfer the basket to the Ninja Foodi Digital Air Fryer Oven and close the door.
4. Select "Air Crisp" mode by rotating the dial.
5. Press the TEMP button and change the value to 375 degrees F.
6. Press the TIME button and change the value to 12 minutes, then press START to begin cooking.
7. Toss the apple slices once cooked halfway through, then resume cooking.
8. Beat yogurt with honey and almond butter in a bowl.
9. Serve the apple chips with the yogurt dip.

Serving Suggestion: Serve the chips with apple sauce.

Variation Tip: Coat the apple slices with breadcrumbs before cooking.

Nutritional Information Per Serving:

Calories 104 | Fat 3g |Sodium 216mg | Carbs 17g | Fiber 3g | Sugar 4g | Protein 1g

Shrimp Spring Rolls

Prep Time: 15 minutes.

Cook Time: 9 minutes.

Serves: 4

Ingredients:

- 2 ½ tablespoons sesame oil
- 2 cups cabbage, shredded
- 1 cup carrots, julienned
- 1 cup red bell pepper, julienned
- 4 oz. raw shrimp, peeled, deveined, chopped
- 3/4 cup snow peas peeled, deveined
- 1/4 cup cilantro, chopped
- 1 tablespoon fresh lime juice
- 2 teaspoons fish sauce
- 1/4 teaspoon crushed red pepper
- 8 (8-inch-square) spring roll wrappers
- 1/2 cup sweet chili sauce

Preparation:

1. Sauté cabbage, bell pepper, and carrots with oil in a cooking pan for 2 minutes.
2. Allow the veggies to cool, then transfer to a bowl.
3. Stir in lime juice, cilantro, snow peas, shrimp, fish sauce, and crushed red pepper, then mix well.
4. Spread the spring roll wrappers on a working surface.
5. Divide the cabbage filling at the center of each wrapper.
6. Wet the edges of the wrappers, fold the top and bottom of each wrapper then roll them.
7. Place the shrimp spring rolls in the Ninja Air Fryer basket.
8. Transfer the basket to the Ninja Foodi Digital Air Fryer Oven and close the door.
9. Select "Air Crisp" mode by rotating the dial.
10. Press the TEMP button and change the value to 390 degrees F.
11. Press the TIME button and change the value to 7 minutes, then press START to begin cooking.
12. Flip the rolls once cooked halfway through, then resume cooking.
13. Serve the rolls with chili sauce.

Serving Suggestion: Serve the rolls with chili sauce or mayonnaise dip.

Variation Tip: Added shredded cheese to the spring roll filling.

Nutritional Information Per Serving:

Calories 180 | Fat 9g |Sodium 318mg | Carbs 19g | Fiber 5g | Sugar 3g | Protein 7g

Curry Chickpeas

Prep Time: 15 minutes.

Cook Time: 15 minutes.

Serves: 6

Ingredients:

- 1 (15-oz.) can chickpeas, drained
- 2 tablespoons red wine vinegar
- 2 tablespoons olive oil
- 2 teaspoons curry powder
- 1/2 teaspoon ground turmeric
- 1/4 teaspoon ground coriander
- 1/4 teaspoon ground cumin
- 1/4 teaspoon 1ground cinnamon
- 1/4 teaspoon salt
- 1/2 teaspoon Aleppo pepper

Preparation:

1. Slightly smash the chickpeas in a bowl with your hands only to remove their skins.
2. Add oil, vinegar, curry powder, coriander, turmeric, cinnamon, and cumin.
3. Toss well and spread the chickpeas in the Ninja Air Fryer basket.
4. Transfer the basket to the Ninja Foodi Digital Air Fryer Oven and close the door.
5. Select "Air Crisp" mode by rotating the dial.
6. Press the TEMP button and change the value to 400 degrees F.
7. Press the TIME button and change the value to 15 minutes, then press START to begin cooking.
8. Toss the chickpeas once cooked halfway through, then resume cooking.
9. Garnish with salt and Aleppo pepper.
10. Serve.

Serving Suggestion: Serve the chickpeas with crumbled nacho chips on top and a cream cheese dip on the side.

Variation Tip: Toss chickpeas with shredded parmesan before cooking.

Nutritional Information Per Serving:

Calories 173 | Fat 8g |Sodium 146mg | Carbs 18g | Fiber 5g | Sugar 1g | Protein 7g

Pork Dumplings

Prep Time: 15 minutes.

Cook Time: 21 minutes.

Serves: 9

Ingredients:

- 1 teaspoon canola oil
- 4 cups bok choy, chopped
- 1 tablespoon fresh ginger, chopped
- 1 tablespoon garlic, chopped
- 4 oz. ground pork
- 1/4 teaspoon crushed red pepper
- 18 (3 1/2-inch-square) dumpling wrappers
- Cooking spray
- 2 tablespoons rice vinegar
- 2 teaspoons soy sauce
- 1 teaspoon toasted sesame oil
- 1/2 teaspoon packed brown sugar
- 1 tablespoon scallions, chopped

Preparation:

1. Sauté bok coy with canola oil in a skillet for 8 minutes.
2. Stir in garlic and ginger and cook for 1 minute.
3. Transfer the bok choy to a plate lined with a paper towel.
4. Mix bok choy mixture with ground pork and red pepper in a medium bowl.
5. Spread the dumpling wrappers on the working surface.
6. Divide the pork mixture at the center of each wrapper.
7. Wet the edges of the wrappers with water and fold the wrappers in half.
8. Pinch the edges of each wrapper and place them in the Ninja Air Fryer basket.
9. Transfer the basket to the Ninja Foodi Digital Air Fryer Oven and close the door.
10. Select "Air Crisp" mode by rotating the dial.
11. Press the TEMP button and change the value to 375 degrees F.
12. Press the TIME button and change the value to 12 minutes, then press START to begin cooking.
13. Flip the dumplings once cooked halfway through, then resume cooking.
14. Meanwhile, mix rice vinegar, sesame oil, soy sauce, scallions and brown sugar in a bowl.
15. Serve the pork dumplings with the prepared sauce.

Serving Suggestion: Serve the dumplings with chili sauce or mayo dip.

Variation Tip: Add shredded cheese to the filling.

Nutritional Information Per Serving:

Calories 140 | Fat 5g |Sodium 244mg | Carbs 16g | Fiber 1g | Sugar 1g | Protein 17g

Spanakopita Bites

Prep Time: 15 minutes.

Cook Time: 17 minutes.

Serves: 6

Ingredients:

- 1 (10-oz.) package spinach leaves
- 2 tablespoons water
- 1/4 cup cottage cheese
- 1 oz. feta cheese, crumbled
- 2 tablespoons Parmesan cheese, grated
- 1 large egg white
- 1 teaspoon lemon zest
- 1 teaspoon dried oregano
- 1/4 teaspoon black pepper
- 1/4 teaspoon salt
- 1/8 teaspoon cayenne pepper
- 4 (13x18 inches) sheets frozen phyllo dough, thawed
- 1 tablespoon olive oil
- Cooking spray

Preparation:

1. Boil spinach in a large pot with boiling pot for 5 minutes, then drain.
2. Mix the spinach with cottage cheese, Parmesan, feta cheese, zest, egg white, oregano, salt, black pepper, and cayenne pepper in a medium bowl.
3. Spread 1 phyllo sheet on a working surface brush the top with oil.
4. Place the second sheet on top and brush it with oil and repeat the layers with the remaining two sheets.
5. Cut these sheets into eight (2 ¼ inch wide) strips. Cut each strip in half and add a tablespoon of the filling at a short end of each strip.
6. Fold the corner covering the filling and make a triangle, then pinch the edges to seal the filling.
7. Place half of the triangles in the Ninja Air Fryer basket and spray them with cooking spray.
8. Transfer the basket to the Ninja Foodi Digital Air Fryer Oven and close the door.
9. Select "Air Crisp" mode by rotating the dial.
10. Press the TEMP button and change the value to 375 degrees F.

11. Press the TIME button and change the value to 12 minutes, then press START to begin cooking.

12. Flip the triangles once cooked halfway through, then resume cooking.

13. Cooking the remaining triangles in the same way.

14. Serve warm.

Serving Suggestion: Serve the Spanakopita with spinach or cream cheese dip.

Variation Tip: Add shredded cooked chicken to the spinach filling.

Nutritional Information Per Serving:

Calories 82 | Fat 4g |Sodium 232mg | Carbs 7g | Fiber 1g | Sugar 0g | Protein 4g

Pita Pizzas

Prep Time: 15 minutes.

Cook Time: 5 minutes.

Serves: 2

Ingredients:

- 1/4 cup marinara sauce
- 2 whole-wheat pita rounds
- 1 cup baby spinach leaves
- 1 plum tomato, sliced
- 1 garlic clove, sliced
- 1 oz. mozzarella cheese, shredded
- 1/4 oz. Parmigiano-Reggiano cheese shaved

Preparation:

1. Place the pita bread in the Ninja baking tray.
2. Spread the marinara sauce on top of both the pita bread.
3. Divide the spinach leaves, tomato slices, garlic, and both kinds of cheese.
4. Transfer the tray to the Ninja Foodi Digital Air Fryer Oven and close the door.
5. Select the "Bake" mode by rotating the dial.
6. Press the TEMP button and change the value to 350 degrees F.
7. Press the TIME button and change the value to 5 minutes, then press START to begin cooking.
8. Serve warm.

Serving Suggestion: Serve the pizza with tomato sauce or mayo dip.

Variation Tip: Add pepperoni and olive slices to the toppings.

Nutritional Information Per Serving:

Calories 229 | Fat 5g |Sodium 510mg | Carbs 37g | Fiber 5g | Sugar 4g | Protein 11g

Corn on the Cob

Prep Time: 15 minutes.

Cook Time: 14 minutes.

Serves: 4

Ingredients:

- 4 corn ears, shucked
- Cooking spray
- 1 ½ tablespoon unsalted butter
- 2 teaspoons garlic, chopped
- 1 teaspoon lime zest
- 1 tablespoon lime juice
- ½ teaspoon salt
- ½ teaspoon black pepper
- 2 tablespoons chopped fresh cilantro

Preparation:

1. Place the corn cobs in the Ninja Air Fryer basket and spray them with cooking spray.
2. Transfer the basket to the Ninja Foodi Digital Air Fryer Oven and close the door.
3. Select "Air Crisp" mode by rotating the dial.
4. Press the TEMP button and change the value to 400 degrees F.
5. Press the TIME button and change the value to 14 minutes, then press START to begin cooking.
6. Flip the corn cobs once cooked halfway through, then resume cooking.
7. Mix butter with salt, black pepper, cilantro, lime zest, lime juice, and garlic in a bowl.
8. Pour this mixture over the corn cobs.
9. Serve warm.

Serving Suggestion: Serve the corn cobs with garlic butter.

Variation Tip: Drizzle paprika on top for more spice.

Nutritional Information Per Serving:

Calories 201 | Fat 7g |Sodium 269mg | Carbs 35g | Fiber 4g | Sugar 12g | Protein 6g

Calzones

Prep Time: 15 minutes.

Cook Time: 14 minutes.

Serves: 4

Ingredients:

- 1 teaspoon olive oil
- 1/4 cup red onion, chopped
- 3 oz. baby spinach leaves
- 1/3 cup marinara sauce
- 2 oz. cooked chicken breast, shredded
- 6 oz. whole-wheat pizza dough
- 1 ½ oz. mozzarella cheese, shredded
- Cooking spray

Preparation:

1. Sauté onion with oil in a skillet for 2 minutes, then add spinach.
2. Cook for 1 ½ minute, then remove it from the heat.
3. Add chicken and marinara sauce, then mix well.
4. Cut the dough into 4 pieces and roll each piece into 6 inches circle.
5. Divide the spinach filling at the center of each dough piece.
6. Top the filling with the cheese and fold the dough in half.
7. Crimp the edges of each calzone and place them in the Ninja Air Fryer basket.
8. Transfer the basket to the Ninja Foodi Digital Air Fryer Oven and close the door.
9. Select "Air Crisp" mode by rotating the dial.
10. Press the TEMP button and change the value to 325 degrees F.
11. Press the TIME button and change the value to 12 minutes, then press START to begin cooking.
12. Flip the calzones once cooked halfway through, then resume cooking.
13. Serve warm.

Serving Suggestion: Serve the calzones with chili garlic sauce.

Variation Tip: Add pepperoni and sliced olives to the filling.

Nutritional Information Per Serving:

Calories 348 | Fat 12g |Sodium 710mg | Carbs 44g | Fiber 5g | Sugar 3g | Protein 11g

Sweet Potato Fries

Prep Time: 15 minutes.

Cook Time: 10 minutes.

Serves: 6

Ingredients:

- 3 sweet potatoes, cut into fries
- 2 tablespoons olive oil
- 1/2 teaspoon salt
- 1/4 teaspoon black pepper
- 1/4 teaspoon paprika
- 1/2 teaspoon garlic powder
- Parsley, to garnish

Preparation:

1. Toss the sweet potatoes with olive oil, salt, black pepper, paprika, and garlic powder in a bowl.
2. Spread the sweet potatoes in the Ninja Air Fryer basket and spray them with cooking spray.
3. Transfer the basket to the Ninja Foodi Digital Air Fryer Oven and close the door.
4. Select "Air Crisp" mode by rotating the dial.
5. Press the TEMP button and change the value to 400 degrees F.
6. Press the TIME button and change the value to 10 minutes, then press START to begin cooking.
7. Toss the fries once cooked halfway through, then resume cooking.
8. Serve warm.

Serving Suggestion: Serve the chips with tomato ketchup.

Variation Tip: Coat the sweet potatoes in breadcrumbs before cooking.

Nutritional Information Per Serving:

Calories 175 | Fat 16g |Sodium 255mg | Carbs 31g | Fiber 1.2g | Sugar 5g | Protein 4.1g

Poultry Mains

Turkey Croquettes

Prep Time: 15 minutes.

Cook Time: 10 minutes.

Serves: 4

Ingredients:

- 1 cup turkey breast, diced
- 2 large eggs
- 1/2 cup potato starch
- 1 cup Japanese style panko
- 1 cup turkey gravy
- 1/2 cup leftover cranberry sauce

Preparation:

1. Beat eggs in a bowl, spread potato starch in another bowl and add panko to a shallow tray.
2. Coat the turkey cubes with potato starch then dip in the eggs and then coat with the panko.
3. Place the turkey cubes in the Ninja Air Fryer basket and spray them with cooking spray.
4. Transfer the basket to the Ninja Foodi Digital Air Fryer Oven and close the door.
5. Select "Air Crisp" mode by rotating the dial.
6. Press the TEMP button and change the value to 380 degrees F.
7. Press the TIME button and change the value to 10 minutes, then press START to begin cooking.
8. Serve with gravy and cranberry sauce.

Serving Suggestion: Serve the turkey croquettes with a kale salad on the side.

Variation Tip: Coat the croquettes with coconut shreds.

Nutritional Information Per Serving:

Calories 235 | Fat 25g |Sodium 122mg | Carbs 23g | Fiber 0.4g | Sugar 1g | Protein 33g

Thanksgiving Turkey Meal

Prep Time: 15 minutes.

Cook Time: 20 minutes.

Serves: 8

Ingredients:

- 1 teaspoon salt
- 1 teaspoon dried thyme
- 1 teaspoon ground rosemary
- 1/2 teaspoon black pepper
- 1/2 teaspoon dried sage
- 1/2 teaspoon garlic powder
- 1/2 teaspoon paprika
- 1/2 teaspoon dark brown sugar
- 2 1/2 lbs. bone-in, skin-on turkey breast
- Olive oil, for brushing

Preparation:

1. Mix salt, thyme, rosemary, black pepper, sage, garlic powder, paprika, and sugar in a bowl.
2. Rub oil and spice blend over the turkey breast.
3. Place the turkey breast the Ninja sheet pan.
4. Transfer the sheet pan to the Ninja Foodi Digital Air Fryer Oven and close the door.
5. Select "Air Roast" mode by rotating the dial.
6. Press the TEMP button and change the value to 360 degrees F.
7. Press the TIME button and change the value to 20 minutes, then press START to begin cooking.
8. Slice and serve warm.

Serving Suggestion: Serve the turkey with roasted green beans and mashed potatoes.

Variation Tip: Place bacon slices on top of the turkey before baking.

Nutritional Information Per Serving:

Calories 235 | Fat 5g |Sodium 422mg | Carbs 16g | Fiber 0g | Sugar 1g | Protein 25g

Italian Turkey Breast

Prep Time: 15 minutes.

Cook Time: 55 minutes.

Serves: 8

Ingredients:

- 1 (4 lbs.) bone-in turkey breast, ribs removed
- 1½ cups Italian dressing
- ¼ cup Worcestershire sauce

Preparation:

1. Cut out the ribs from the turkey breast and rub it with Italian seasoning and Worcestershire sauce.
2. Place the turkey on a plate, cover, and refrigerate for 1 hour for marination.
3. Place the marinated turkey breasts in the Ninja Air Fryer basket.
4. Transfer the basket to the Ninja Foodi Digital Air Fryer Oven and close the door.
5. Select "Air Crisp" mode by rotating the dial.
6. Press the TEMP button and change the value to 350 degrees F.
7. Press the TIME button and change the value to 20 minutes, then press START to begin cooking.
8. Flip the turkey breast and continue cooking for another 35 minutes.
9. Slice and serve warm.

Serving Suggestion: Serve the turkey breast with roasted veggies.

Variation Tip: wrap the turkey breast with bacon slices before baking.

Nutritional Information Per Serving:

Calories 369 | Fat 14g |Sodium 442mg | Carbs 13.3g | Fiber 0.4g | Sugar 2g | Protein 32.3g

Turkey Meatloaf

Prep Time: 15 minutes.

Cook Time: 32 minutes.

Serves: 6

Ingredients:

- Cooking spray
- 1/4 cup water
- Salt, as desired
- 1 lb. uncooked ground turkey
- 1/3 cup panko bread crumbs
- 2 potatoes, peeled, cut into 1-inch pieces
- 1 yellow onion, peeled, grated
- 1 garlic clove, peeled, grated
- 1 egg
- 1/4 cup Colby-Jack cheese, diced
- 1/3 cup ketchup
- Ground black pepper, to taste
- 1 package (12 oz.) fresh green beans
- 1 tablespoon olive oil
- 1/3 cup whole milk
- 1 tablespoon butter

Preparation:

1. Add potatoes onto a large piece of aluminum foil and season them with cooking spray and salt.

2. Wrap the potatoes and place the packet in the Ninja sheet pan.

3. Mix turkey with egg, cheese, half the ketchup, black pepper, salt, egg, garlic, onion, and breadcrumbs in a bowl.

4. Divide the meatloaves mixture into four portions.

5. Shape each portion into a mini-loaf, brush the ketchup on top and place them in the sheet pan.

6. Transfer the sheet pan to the Ninja Foodi Digital Air Fryer Oven and close the door.

7. Select "Air Roast" mode by rotating the dial.

8. Press the TEMP button and change the value to 400 degrees F.

9. Press the TIME button and change the value to 15 minutes, then press START to begin cooking.

10. Meanwhile, toss green beans with salt, black pepper and olive oil in a bowl.

11. Place green beans in the sheet pan and return it to the Ninja Digital Air Fryer oven.

12. Continue cooking for another 17 minutes on the same mode and temperature.

13. Unwrap the potatoes and add them to a bowl.

14. Mash the potatoes and add milk, black pepper, salt and milk.

15. Mix well and serve the turkey loaves and green beans.

16. Serve warm.

Serving Suggestion: Serve the meatloaf with fresh cucumber and couscous salad.

Variation Tip: Wrap the meatloaves with bacon slices before cooking.

Nutritional Information Per Serving:

Calories 453 | Fat 2.4g |Sodium 216mg | Carbs 18g | Fiber 2.3g | Sugar 1.2g | Protein 23.2g

General Tso's Chicken

Prep Time: 15 minutes.

Cook Time: 17 minutes.

Serves: 4

Ingredients:

- 1 large egg
- 1 lb. chicken thighs, cut into chunks
- 1/3 cup 2 teaspoons cornstarch
- ¼ teaspoon salt
- ¼ teaspoon ground white pepper
- 7 tablespoons chicken broth
- 2 tablespoons soy sauce
- 2 tablespoons ketchup
- 2 teaspoons sugar
- 2 teaspoons rice vinegar
- 1 ½ tablespoon canola oil
- 4 chiles de árbol, chopped
- 1 tablespoon fresh ginger, chopped
- 1 tablespoon garlic, chopped
- 2 tablespoons green onion, sliced
- 1 teaspoon toasted sesame oil
- ½ teaspoon toasted sesame seeds

Preparation:

1. Beat egg in a bowl and add chicken to coat well.
2. Mix 1/3 cup cornstarch with black pepper and salt in a bowl.
3. Coat the chicken with the cornstarch mixture.
4. Place the chicken in the Ninja Air Fryer basket and spray with cooking spray.
5. Transfer the basket to the Ninja Foodi Digital Air Fryer Oven and close the door.
6. Select "Air Roast" mode by rotating the dial.
7. Press the TEMP button and change the value to 400 degrees F.
8. Press the TIME button and change the value to 16 minutes, then press START to begin cooking.
9. Flip the chicken once cooked halfway through and resume cooking.
10. Mix 2 teaspoons with broth, soy sauce, sugar, rice vinegar, ketchup, and 2 teaspoons cornstarch in a bowl.
11. Sauté chiles with oil in a skillet for 30 seconds.

12. Stir in ginger and garlic then sauté for 30 seconds.

13. Add cornstarch sauté to the garlic and cook until the mixture thickens.

14. Stir in air fried chicken then mix well.

15. Garnish with sesame oil, sesame seeds and green onion.

16. Serve warm.

Serving Suggestion: Serve the chicken with fresh herbs on top and a bowl of steamed rice.

Variation Tip: Use honey or maple syrup to the sauce if not using ketchup.

Nutritional Information Per Serving:

Calories 302 | Fat 13g |Sodium 611mg | Carbs 18g | Fiber 0g | Sugar g4 | Protein 26g

Chicken Enchiladas

Prep Time: 15 minutes.
Cook Time: 15 minutes.
Serves: 12

Ingredients:

- 12 corn tortillas
- 1½ cups Mexican chicken, shredded
- 2 cups enchilada sauce
- 1½ cups Mexican cheese, shredded

Preparation:

1. Spread six tortillas in the Ninja sheet pan and spray them with cooking spray.
2. Transfer the sheet pan to the Ninja Foodi Digital Air Fryer Oven and close the door.
3. Select "Air Crisp" mode by rotating the dial.
4. Press the TEMP button and change the value to 425 degrees F.
5. Press the TIME button and change the value to 5 minutes, then press START to begin cooking.
6. Air Fry the remaining tortillas in the same manner.
7. Mix shredded chicken with enchilada sauce in a bowl.
8. Divide the filling in each tortilla then place the stuffed tortillas in the Ninja sheet pan.
9. Drizzle sheet on top of each tortilla.
10. Transfer the sheet pan to the Ninja Foodi Digital Air Fryer Oven and close the door.
11. Select the "Bake" mode by rotating the dial.
12. Press the TEMP button and change the value to 325 degrees F.
13. Press the TIME button and change the value to 15 minutes, then press START to begin cooking.
14. Serve warm.

Serving Suggestion: Serve the chicken enchiladas with toasted bread slices.

Variation Tip: Add corn kernels to the chicken filling.

Nutritional Information Per Serving:
Calories 354 | Fat 25g |Sodium 412mg | Carbs 22.3g | Fiber 0.2g | Sugar 1g | Protein 28.3g

Korean Chicken Wings

Prep Time: 15 minutes.

Cook Time: 10 minutes.

Serves: 6

Ingredients:

- 2 lbs. chicken wings
- 2 tablespoons of rice wine
- 1 teaspoon onion powder
- 1 teaspoon garlic powder
- 1 teaspoon sea salt
- 1/4 teaspoon ginger powder
- Black pepper, to taste

Soy Garlic Sauce

- 3 tablespoons soy sauce
- 2 tablespoons water
- 2 tablespoons of rice wine
- 2 tablespoons brown sugar
- 2 tablespoons honey
- 1/2 tablespoon ginger, minced
- ½ tablespoon garlic, minced
- 1 teaspoon ground black peppers
- 1 oz. green onions, chopped
- 3 dried chilies, chopped
- 2 teaspoons corn starch
- 2 teaspoons water

Sweet Spicy Sauce

- 1 ½ tablespoons ketchup
- 1 tablespoon Korean chili paste
- 2 tablespoons honey
- 2 tablespoons brown sugar
- 1 tablespoon soy sauce
- 1 tablespoon minced garlic
- ½ tablespoons sesame oil

Garnish

- Sesame seeds

- Green onion, sliced

Preparation:

1. Dip the chicken wings in the rice wine and soak for 5 minutes.
2. Mix black peppers, ginger powder, salt, garlic powder and onion powder in a bowl.
3. Add the chicken wings and coat them well with the spices.
4. Spread the chicken wings in the Ninja Air Fryer basket and spray them with the cooking spray.
5. Transfer the basket to the Ninja Foodi Digital Air Fryer Oven and close the door.
6. Select "Air Crisp" mode by rotating the dial.
7. Press the TEMP button and change the value to 400 degrees F.
8. Press the TIME button and change the value to 10 minutes, then press START to begin cooking.
9. Toss the chicken once cooked halfway through.
10. Meanwhile, mix all the soy garlic sauce in a cooking pot and cook for 2 minutes, then allow it to cool.
11. Mix the sweet and spicy sauce ingredients in a bowl.
12. Add the chicken wings to the soy garlic sauce then mix well.
13. Pour in the sweet and spicy sauce then mix well.
14. Serve.

Serving Suggestion: Serve the wings with white rice or vegetable chow Mein.

Variation Tip: Coat or dust the wings with flour for a crispy texture.

Nutritional Information Per Serving:
Calories 297 | Fat 14g |Sodium 364mg | Carbs 8g | Fiber 1g | Sugar 3g | Protein 32g

Cheesy Chicken Nachos

Prep Time: 15 minutes.

Cook Time: 25 minutes.

Serves: 4

Ingredients:

- 1 lb. chicken breasts, cut into cubes
- 1 tablespoon olive oil
- 8 oz. tortilla chips
- 1 can (15 ½ oz.) black beans
- 2 cups cheddar cheese, shredded
- 1 cup Mexican blend cheese, shredded

Nacho seasoning

- 1 tablespoon fresh lemon juice
- 1 tablespoon fresh lime juice
- 1 teaspoon ground cumin
- ¼ cup cilantro, chopped
- 1 teaspoon onion powder
- 2 teaspoons chili powder
- 1 teaspoon salt

Preparation:

1. Mix all the nacho seasoning ingredients in a bowl.
2. Toss chicken with nacho seasoning and oil in the Ninja sheet pan.
3. Transfer the sheet pan to the Ninja Foodi Digital Air Fryer Oven and close the door.
4. Select "Air Roast" mode by rotating the dial.
5. Press the TEMP button and change the value to 350 degrees F.
6. Press the TIME button and change the value to 15 minutes, then press START to begin cooking.
7. Spread the tortilla chips in a sheet pan and top them with chicken, black beans, and cheese.
8. Transfer the basket to the Ninja Foodi Digital Air Fryer Oven and close the door.
9. Select "Air Roast" mode by rotating the dial.
10. Press the TEMP button and change the value to 350 degrees F.
11. Press the TIME button and change the value to 10 minutes, then press START to begin cooking.
12. Serve warm.

Serving Suggestion: Serve the nachos with avocado guacamole.

Variation Tip: Add corn kernels to the nachos topping.

Nutritional Information Per Serving:

Calories 352 | Fat 14g |Sodium 220mg | Carbs 16g | Fiber 0.2g | Sugar 1g | Protein 26g

Chicken Stir-Fry

Prep Time: 15 minutes.

Cook Time: 30 minutes.

Serves: 2

Ingredients:

- 1 lb. chicken breasts, cut into cubes
- 1 red bell pepper, sliced
- 1 yellow bell pepper, sliced
- 1 orange bell pepper, sliced
- 2 carrots, sliced
- ½ cup stir-fry sauce
- 1 head broccoli, cut into florets
- 1 teaspoon sesame seeds

Preparation:

1. Toss chicken, carrots, and peppers in the Ninja sheet pan.
2. Transfer the sheet pan to the Ninja Foodi Digital Air Fryer Oven and close the door.
3. Select "Air Roast" mode by rotating the dial.
4. Press the TEMP button and change the value to 400 degrees F.
5. Press the TIME button and change the value to 20 minutes, then press START to begin cooking.
6. After 10 minutes of cooking, add broccoli then return the pan to the Ninja Foodi digital Air Fryer oven.
7. Resume cooking for another 10 minutes.
8. Garnish with sesame seeds.
9. Serve warm.

Serving Suggestion: Serve the chicken fry inside warmed pita bread.

Variation Tip: Add canned corns to the stir fry.

Nutritional Information Per Serving:

Calories 388 | Fat 8g |Sodium 339mg | Carbs 8g | Fiber 1g | Sugar 2g | Protein 13g

Honey Lime Chicken Wings

Prep Time: 15 minutes.

Cook Time: 25 minutes.

Serves: 4

Ingredients:

- 3 tablespoons sriracha sauce
- ¼ cup honey
- 2 tablespoons soy sauce
- 1 tablespoon brown sugar
- 1 tablespoon ground ginger
- Zest and juice of 2 limes
- 2 ½ lbs. chicken wings

Preparation:

1. Whisk sriracha sauce, honey, soy sauce, brown sugar, ginger, lime zest, and lime juice in a bowl.
2. Add the chicken to the bowl and mix well to coat.
3. Cover the chicken and refrigerate for 1 hour or more to marinate.
4. Place the chicken wings in the Ninja Air Fryer basket and spray them with cooking spray.
5. Transfer the basket to the Ninja Foodi Digital Air Fryer Oven and close the door.
6. Select "Air Crisp" mode by rotating the dial.
7. Press the TEMP button and change the value to 400 degrees F.
8. Press the TIME button and change the value to 25 minutes, then press START to begin cooking.
9. Toss the chicken wings once cooked halfway through, then resume cooking.
10. Serve warm.

Serving Suggestion: Serve the chicken wings with steaming white rice.

Variation Tip: Add 1 tbsp tahini to the seasoning and marinate.

Nutritional Information Per Serving:
Calories 301 | Fat 16g |Sodium 189mg | Carbs 32g | Fiber 0.3g | Sugar 0.1g | Protein 28.2g

Chicken Tenders

Prep Time: 15 minutes.

Cook Time: 13 minutes.

Serves: 4

Ingredients:

- 1 lb. chicken tenderloins
- ½ cup flour
- 2 eggs, beaten
- ⅓ cup Italian breadcrumbs
- ⅓ cup Parmesan cheese, grated
- ½ teaspoons garlic salt
- ½ teaspoons black pepper
- olive oil spray

Preparation:

1. Spread the flour in a bowl, mix breadcrumbs with parmesan cheese, garlic salt, and black pepper in another bowl.
2. Beat eggs with black pepper and salt in a third bowl.
3. Coat the chicken tenders with the flour, then dip them in the eggs and coat them with breadcrumbs mixture.
4. Place the chicken tenders in the Ninja Air Fryer basket and spray them with cooking spray.
5. Transfer the basket to the Ninja Foodi Digital Air Fryer Oven and close the door.
6. Select "Air Crisp" mode by rotating the dial.
7. Press the TEMP button and change the value to 400 degrees F.
8. Press the TIME button and change the value to 13 minutes, then press START to begin cooking.
9. Toss the coated chicken tenders once cooked halfway through and resume cooking.
10. Serve warm.

Serving Suggestion: Serve the chicken tenders with chili garlic sauce.

Variation Tip: Add dried herbs to the flour for seasoning.

Nutritional Information Per Serving:

Calories 231 | Fat 20g |Sodium 941mg | Carbs 30g | Fiber 0.9g | Sugar 1.4g | Protein 14.6g

Chicken, Sweet Potatoes and Broccoli

Prep Time: 15 minutes.

Cook Time: 22 minutes.

Serves: 4

Ingredients:

- 3 tablespoons olive oil
- 1 tablespoon Cajun seasoning
- 1 head broccoli, cut into florets
- 1 teaspoon salt
- 1 lb. boneless chicken breasts, cut into cubes
- 2 medium sweet potatoes, peeled, cut into cubes
- 1 teaspoon ground black pepper

Preparation:

1. Toss chicken, broccoli and sweet potatoes with Cajun seasoning and 1 tablespoon oil in the Ninja sheet pan.
2. Transfer the sheet pan to the Ninja Foodi Digital Air Fryer Oven and close the door.
3. Select "Air Roast" mode by rotating the dial.
4. Press the TEMP button and change the value to 415 degrees F.
5. Press the TIME button and change the value to 22 minutes, then press START to begin cooking.
6. Serve warm.

Serving Suggestion: Serve the chicken broccoli with a fresh crouton's salad.

Variation Tip: Add a drizzle of cheese on top.

Nutritional Information Per Serving:

Calories 440 | Fat 7.9g |Sodium 581mg | Carbs 21.8g | Fiber 2.6g | Sugar 7g | Protein 37.2g

Chicken Sheet Pan Meal

Prep Time: 15 minutes.

Cook Time: 35 minutes.

Serves: 4

Ingredients:

- ¼ cup olive oil
- 1 teaspoon sea salt
- ½ teaspoons black pepper
- 12 oz. red potatoes, diced
- 2 medium zucchinis, diced
- 1 medium yellow squash, diced
- 1 red onion, diced
- 1 bulb garlic, peeled and minced

- 16 oz. chicken breast, diced
- 8 sprigs rosemary fresh
- 3 lemons, sliced

Preparation:

1. Toss chicken with olive oil, salt, black pepper, garlic, rosemary, squash, and zucchini in a large bowl.
2. Spread the potatoes in the Ninja sheet pan.
3. Transfer the sheet pan to the Ninja Foodi Digital Air Fryer Oven and close the door.
4. Select "Air Roast" mode by rotating the dial.
5. Press the TEMP button and change the value to 450 degrees F.
6. Press the TIME button and change the value to 10 minutes, then press START to begin cooking.
7. Add chicken, zucchini, onion, garlic, and squash to the sheet pan.
8. Drizzle black pepper, salt, and oil over the chicken and veggies.
9. Return the sheet pan to the Ninja Digital Air Fryer oven.
10. Select "Air Crisp" mode by rotating the dial.
11. Press the TEMP button and change the value to 325 degrees F.
12. Press the TIME button and change the value to 25 minutes, then press START to begin cooking.
13. Serve warm.

Serving Suggestion: Serve the sheet pan meal with tomato sauce and toasted bread slices.

Variation Tip: Add butter sauce on top of the veggies before cooking.

Nutritional Information Per Serving:

Calories 419 | Fat 13g |Sodium 432mg | Carbs 9.1g | Fiber 3g | Sugar 1g | Protein 33g

Turkey Ham Casserole

Prep Time: 15 minutes.

Cook Time: 35 minutes.

Serves: 8

Ingredients:

- 1 2/3 oz. butter
- 3 leeks, sliced
- 1 oz. plain flour
- ½ cup white wine
- 2 cups chicken stock
- ½ cup double cream
- 1 lb. cooked turkey, diced
- 5 oz. ham, diced
- 2 tarragon sprigs, leaves finely chopped
- 3 ½ oz. peas, defrosted
- 6 cubes of frozen spinach, defrosted
- Salt and black pepper, to taste

Crust:

- 3 ½ oz. breadcrumbs
- 1 small onion, grated
- 3 ½ oz. chestnuts, grated
- 1 oz. dried cranberries, soaked in warm water (optional)
- 2 teaspoons dried sage
- Small bunch of parsley, finely chopped
- 1 large knob of butter

Preparation:

1. Sauté butter with leeks and seasoning in a skillet until soft.
2. Stir in flour and mix well. Pour in stock and cream, then mix well.
3. Add ham, turkey, tarragon, and peas, then mix until sauce until its sauce thickens.
4. Add spinach, black pepper, and salt, then mix well.
5. Spread this leek mixture in a casserole dish and top it with breadcrumbs, chestnuts, herbs, cranberries, and onion.
6. Add butter, black pepper, and salt on top of the casserole.
7. Transfer the casserole dish to the Ninja Foodi Digital Air Fryer Oven and close the door.
8. Select the "Bake" mode by rotating the dial.

9. Press the TEMP button and change the value to 350 degrees F.

10. Press the TIME button and change the value to 30 minutes, then press START to begin cooking.

11. Serve warm.

Serving Suggestion: Serve the casserole with roasted veggies on the side.

Variation Tip: Add peas and corn to the casserole.

Nutritional Information Per Serving:

Calories 334 | Fat 16g |Sodium 462mg | Carbs 31g | Fiber 0.4g | Sugar 3g | Protein 35.3g

Beef, Pork, and Lamb

Italian Pasta Bake

Prep Time: 15 minutes.

Cook Time: 57 minutes.

Serves: 6

Ingredients:

- 2 lbs. ground beef
- 1 large onion, chopped
- 2 garlic cloves, minced
- 1 can (14 ½ oz.) tomatoes, diced, undrained
- 1 teaspoon Italian seasoning
- 3 cups pasta shells
- 1 jar (24 oz.) spaghetti sauce
- 3 plum tomatoes, sliced
- 3/4 cup provolone cheese, shredded
- 1 can (4 oz.) mushroom, drained
- 3/4 cup mozzarella cheese, shredded

Preparation:

1. Sauté beef and onion with oil in a skillet for 6 minutes.
2. Stir in garlic and cook for 1 minute.
3. Add Italian seasoning, mushrooms, tomatoes, and spaghetti sauce.
4. Boil and then cook on a simmer for 20 minutes.
5. Meanwhile, boil pasta in a cooking pot according to the instructions.
6. Drain and add pasta to the beef sauce.
7. Spread the beef- pasta in a casserole dish, then add cheese on top.
8. Transfer the sheet pan to the Ninja Foodi Digital Air Fryer Oven and close the door.
9. Select the "Bake" mode by rotating the dial.
10. Press the TEMP button and change the value to 350 degrees F.
11. Press the TIME button and change the value to 30 minutes, then press START to begin cooking.
12. Slice and serve warm.

Serving Suggestion: Serve the casserole with mashed potatoes.

Variation Tip: Use chicken mince instead of beef.

Nutritional Information Per Serving:
Calories 305 | Fat 25g |Sodium 532mg | Carbs 2.3g | Fiber 0.4g | Sugar 2g | Protein 18.3g

Sausage Casserole

Prep Time: 15 minutes.

Cook Time: 55 minutes.

Serves: 8

Ingredients:

- 1 lb. ground pork sausage
- 1 teaspoon mustard powder
- ½ teaspoon salt
- 4 eggs, beaten
- 2 cups of milk
- 6 white bread slices, toasted and cubed
- 8 oz. Cheddar cheese, shredded

Preparation:

1. Sauté sausage in a skillet until brown then keep it aside.
2. Whisk salt, eggs, milk, and mustard powder in a bowl.
3. Spread the bread cubes, sausage in a casserole dish.
4. Pour this mixture on top and drizzle cheese.
5. Cover it with a foil sheet and refrigerate the sausage casserole for 1 hour.
6. Transfer the casserole dish to the Ninja Foodi Digital Air Fryer Oven and close the door.
7. Select the "Bake" mode by rotating the dial.
8. Press the TEMP button and change the value to 350 degrees F.
9. Press the TIME button and change the value to 45 minutes, then press START to begin cooking.
10. Remove the foil and continue baking for another 10 minutes.
11. Serve warm.

Serving Suggestion: Serve the casserole with toasted bread slices.

Variation Tip: Add crumbled bacon on top.

Nutritional Information Per Serving:

Calories 325 | Fat 16g |Sodium 431mg | Carbs 22g | Fiber 1.2g | Sugar 4g | Protein 23g

Christmas Casserole

Prep Time: 15 minutes.

Cook Time: 30 minutes.

Serves: 8

Ingredients:

- 7 eggs
- 1/4 cup milk
- 1 (16 oz.) package biscuit dough, diced
- 1 ½ cups cheddar cheese, shredded
- 4 green onions, chopped
- 8 slices bacon, cooked and chopped

Preparation:

1. Beat eggs with milk in a casserole dish.
2. Add onions, cheese, biscuit pieces, and bacon.
3. Transfer the casserole dish to the Ninja Foodi Digital Air Fryer Oven and close the door.
4. Select the "Bake" mode by rotating the dial.
5. Press the TEMP button and change the value to 350 degrees F.
6. Press the TIME button and change the value to 30 minutes, then press START to begin cooking.
7. Serve warm.

Serving Suggestion: Serve this casserole with pasta or spaghetti.

Variation Tip: Add toasted croutons on top.

Nutritional Information Per Serving:

Calories 425 | Fat 14g |Sodium 411mg | Carbs 44g | Fiber 0.3g | Sugar 1g | Protein 8.3g

Holiday Ham

Prep Time: 15 minutes.

Cook Time: 30 minutes.

Serves: 6

Ingredients:

- 3 lbs. boneless spiral ham

Glaze

- ½ cup honey
- ¼ cup brown sugar
- 2 tablespoons Dijon mustard
- ¼ teaspoons nutmeg
- 1/4 teaspoon cayenne pepper
- ¼ teaspoons salt

Preparation:

1. Wrap the ham in a foil sheet and place it in the Ninja sheet pan.
2. Transfer the sheet pan to the Ninja Foodi Digital Air Fryer Oven and close the door.
3. Select "Air Roast" mode by rotating the dial.
4. Press the TEMP button and change the value to 300 degrees F.
5. Press the TIME button and change the value to 15 minutes, then press START to begin cooking.
6. Mix remaining ingredients for glaze in a saucepan and cook it to a boil with occasional stirring.
7. Unwrap the ham and brush it with the prepared glazed.
8. Return the ham to the Ninja digital Air Fryer oven.
9. Continue roasting the ham for another 15 minutes at 350 degrees F.
10. Slice and serve warm.

Serving Suggestion: Serve the ham with sweet potato casserole.

Variation Tip: Add cheese on top of the ham and then broil after cooking.

Nutritional Information Per Serving:

Calories 425 | Fat 15g |Sodium 345mg | Carbs 12.3g | Fiber 1.4g | Sugar 3g | Protein 23.3g

Pork Meatballs

Prep Time: 15 minutes.

Cook Time: 11 minutes.

Serves: 6

Ingredients:

- 1 ½ lbs. ground pork
- 1 cup plain bread crumbs
- ½ cup milk
- 1 large egg
- ½ cup celery, chopped
- ¼ cup onion, chopped
- 2 tablespoons sage, chopped
- 1 tablespoon rosemary, chopped
- 1 tablespoon thyme leaves
- 1 tablespoon parsley, chopped
- ½ teaspoon salt
- ⅛ teaspoon black pepper

Preparation:

1. Soak breadcrumbs in milk in a large bowl and keep it aside for 5 minutes.
2. Stir in ground pork, egg, celery, onion, sage, rosemary, thyme leaves, parsley, black pepper, and salt.
3. Mix well and make golf-ball sized meatballs out of this mixture.
4. Place the meatballs in the Ninja Air Fryer basket and spray them with cooking spray.
5. Transfer the basket to the Ninja Foodi Digital Air Fryer Oven and close the door.
6. Select "Air Crispy" mode by rotating the dial.
7. Press the TEMP button and change the value to 390 degrees F.
8. Press the TIME button and change the value to 11 minutes, then press START to begin cooking.
9. Toss the meatballs once cooked halfway through, then resume cooking.
10. Serve warm.

Serving Suggestion: Serve the meatballs with mashed potatoes.

Variation Tip: Roll the meatballs in breadcrumbs or crushed cornflakes before baking.

Nutritional Information Per Serving:

Calories 91 | Fat 5g |Sodium 88mg | Carbs 3g | Fiber 0g | Sugar 0g | Protein 7g

Cauliflower Pork Casserole

Prep Time: 15 minutes.

Cook Time: 30 minutes.

Serves: 8

Ingredients:

- 3 (16 oz.) packages frozen cauliflower
- 2 cups sour cream
- 2 cups cheddar cheese, shredded
- 3 teaspoons chicken bouillon granules
- 1 ½ teaspoon ground mustard
- 1/4 cup butter, cubed
- 1 cup pork, minced
- 3/4 cup California walnuts, chopped

Preparation:

1. Boil the cauliflowers in hot water until soft. Drain and transfer the cauliflower to a 13x9 inches casserole dish.
2. Sauté butter with walnuts and pork in a skillet until golden brown.
3. Spread this mixture on top of the cauliflower.
4. Beat sour cream, bouillon, mustard, and cheese in a bowl.
5. Spoon this mixture on top of the cauliflower pork casserole.
6. Transfer the casserole dish to the Ninja Foodi Digital Air Fryer Oven and close the door.
7. Select the "Bake" mode by rotating the dial.
8. Press the TEMP button and change the value to 350 degrees F.
9. Press the TIME button and change the value to 20 minutes, then press START to begin cooking.
10. Serve warm.

Serving Suggestion: Serve the casserole with crispy bacon on top.

Variation Tip: Add a layer of the boiled pasta to the casserole.

Nutritional Information Per Serving:

Calories 276 | Fat 21g |Sodium 476mg | Carbs 12g | Fiber 3g | Sugar 4g | Protein 10g

Balsamic Pork Veggie Meal

Prep Time: 15 minutes.

Cook Time: 30 minutes.

Serves: 4

Ingredients:

- 4 boneless pork chops
- 1 green bell pepper, chopped
- 1 orange bell pepper, chopped
- 8 baby Yukon gold potatoes, chopped
- 1 tablespoon rosemary, minced
- ¼ cup balsamic vinegar
- 1 tablespoon honey
- 2 teaspoons garlic powder
- Salt and black pepper to taste

Preparation:

1. Mix the pork chops with bell pepper, gold potatoes, rosemary, balsamic vinegar, honey, garlic powder, black pepper and salt in the Ninja sheet pan.
2. Transfer the sheet pan to the Ninja Foodi Digital Air Fryer Oven and close the door.
3. Select the "Bake" mode by rotating the dial.
4. Press the TEMP button and change the value to 325 degrees F.
5. Press the TIME button and change the value to 30 minutes, then press START to begin cooking.
6. Serve warm.

Serving Suggestion: Serve the pork meal with fresh greens salad.

Variation Tip: Wrap the pork chops, spices, and vegetables in a foil sheet before baking for a rich taste.

Nutritional Information Per Serving:

Calories 380 | Fat 20g |Sodium 686mg | Carbs 33g | Fiber 1g | Sugar 1.2g | Protein 21g

Sheet Pan Pork with Apples

Prep Time: 15 minutes.

Cook Time: 23 minutes.

Serves: 4

Ingredients:

- 1 medium sweet potato, sliced
- 2 (6 oz.) pork chops
- 1 small apple, sliced
- 6 oz. asparagus
- 2 tablespoons olive oil
- 2 teaspoons bourbon BBQ sauce

Spice Blend

- ½ teaspoons fine grind sea salt
- ½ teaspoons black pepper
- ½ teaspoons cinnamon
- ½ teaspoons chipotle powder

Preparation:

1. Mix spice blend ingredients in a small bowl.
2. Toss sweet potatoes with olive oil and 1/3 spice blend in the Ninja sheet pan.
3. Transfer the sheet pan to the Ninja Foodi Digital Air Fryer Oven and close the door.
4. Select "Air Roast" mode by rotating the dial.
5. Press the TEMP button and change the value to 350 degrees F.
6. Press the TIME button and change the value to 15 minutes, then press START to begin cooking.
7. After 10 minutes, press PAUSE and add asparagus to the sweet potatoes.
8. Drizzle black pepper, oil, and salt over the asparagus and resume cooking.
9. Season pork and apples with the spice blend and BBQ sauce on a bowl.
10. Add the apples and pork to the sweet potatoes in the sheet pan.
11. Transfer the sheet pans to the Ninja Foodi Digital Air Fryer Oven and close the door.
12. Select "Air Crisp" mode by rotating the dial.
13. Press the TEMP button and change the value to 325 degrees F.
14. Press the TIME button and change the value to 8 minutes, then press START to begin cooking.
15. Serve warm.

Serving Suggestion: Serve the pork with boiled rice or spaghetti.

Variation Tip: Use apple sauce for seasoning.

Nutritional Information Per Serving:

Calories 361 | Fat 16g |Sodium 515mg | Carbs 19.3g | Fiber 0.1g | Sugar 18.2g | Protein 33.3g

Lamb Sirloin Steak

Prep Time: 15 minutes.

Cook Time: 15 minutes.

Serves: 2

Ingredients:

- 1/2 onion, chopped
- 4 ginger slices
- 5 garlic cloves, minced
- 1 teaspoon garam masala
- 1 teaspoon ground fennel
- 1 teaspoon ground cinnamon
- 1/2 teaspoon ground cardamom
- 1 teaspoon cayenne pepper
- 1 teaspoon salt
- 1 lb. boneless lamb sirloin steaks

Preparation:

1. Blend ginger, garlic, onion, garam masala, fennel, cinnamon, cardamom, cayenne pepper, and salt in a blender.
2. Place the lamb chops in the Ninja sheet pan and rub the spice blend on both sides.
3. Transfer the sheet pan to the Ninja Foodi Digital Air Fryer Oven and close the door.
4. Select "Air Crisp" mode by rotating the dial.
5. Press the TEMP button and change the value to 330 degrees F.
6. Press the TIME button and change the value to 15 minutes, then press START to begin cooking.
7. Flip the lamb once cooked halfway through, then resume cooking.
8. Serve warm.

Serving Suggestion: Serve the lamb with garlic slices and fresh herbs on top.

Variation Tip: Add butter to the chops before cooking.

Nutritional Information Per Serving:

Calories 405 | Fat 22.7g |Sodium 227mg | Carbs 26.1g | Fiber 1.4g | Sugar 0.9g | Protein 45.2g

Masala Chops

Prep Time: 15 minutes.

Cook Time: 15 minutes.

Serves: 2

Ingredients:

- 1 lb. Lamb chops
- 1 ½ tablespoons red chili powder
- 1 tablespoon turmeric powder
- 1/2 tablespoons garam masala powder
- 1 teaspoon salt
- 1 tablespoon cumin powder
- 1 tablespoon white vinegar
- 2 tablespoons ginger garlic paste
- 3 tablespoons vegetable oil

Preparation:

1. Place the lamb chops in the Ninja Sheet pan.
2. Sauté ginger garlic paste with oil in a skillet until golden.
3. Add rest of the spices, then mix well, then allow it cool.
4. Pour this mixture over the lamb chops and rub it on both sides.
5. Transfer the sheet pan to the Ninja Foodi Digital Air Fryer Oven and close the door.
6. Select "Air Roast" mode by rotating the dial.
7. Press the TEMP button and change the value to 390 degrees F.
8. Press the TIME button and change the value to 10 minutes, then press START to begin cooking.
9. Serve warm.

Serving Suggestion: Serve the chops with boiled peas, carrots, and potatoes on the side.

Variation Tip: Mix the spices with yogurt and marinate the chops in this mixture for 1 hour then bake.

Nutritional Information Per Serving:

Calories 345 | Fat 36g |Sodium 272mg | Carbs 41g | Fiber 0.2g | Sugar 0.1g | Protein 22.5g

Lamb Chops with Garlic Sauce

Prep Time: 15 minutes.

Cook Time: 22 minutes.

Serves: 8

Ingredients:

- 1 garlic bulb
- 3 tablespoons olive oil
- 1 tablespoon oregano, chopped
- Sea salt, to taste
- Black pepper, to taste
- 8 lamb chops

Preparation:

1. Rub the garlic and olive oil over the chops and place them in the Ninja Air Fryer basket.
2. Transfer the basket to the Ninja Foodi Digital Air Fryer Oven and close the door.
3. Select "Air Roast" mode by rotating the dial.
4. Press the TEMP button and change the value to 390 degrees F.
5. Press the TIME button and change the value to 12 minutes, then press START to begin cooking.
6. Transfer the garlic to a bowl and allow it to cool.
7. Mix herbs with olive oil, black pepper and salt in a bowl.
8. Rub this mixture over the lamb chops and marinate for 5 minutes.
9. Squeeze the garlic out of its peel and rub it over the chops.
10. Place the chops in the sheet pan.
11. Transfer the sheet pan to the Ninja Foodi Digital Air Fryer Oven and close the door.
12. Select "Air Crisp" mode by rotating the dial.
13. Press the TEMP button and change the value to 350 degrees F.
14. Press the TIME button and change the value to 10 minutes, then press START to begin cooking.
15. Flip the chops once cooked halfway through and resume cooking.
16. Serve warm.

Serving Suggestion: Serve the chops with sautéed green beans and mashed potatoes.

Variation Tip: Drizzle parmesan cheese on top before cooking.

Nutritional Information Per Serving:

Calories 395 | Fat 9.5g |Sodium 655mg | Carbs 13.4g | Fiber 0.4g | Sugar 0.4g | Protein 28.3g

Herbed Lamb Chops

Prep Time: 15 minutes.

Cook Time: 17 minutes.

Serves: 2

Ingredients:

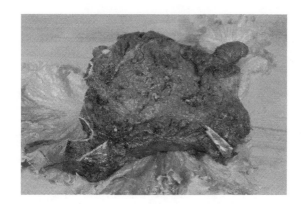

- 1 teaspoon rosemary
- 1 teaspoon thyme
- 1 teaspoon oregano
- 1 teaspoon salt
- 1 teaspoon coriander
- 2 tablespoons olive oil
- 2 tablespoons lemon juice
- 1 lb. lamb chops

Preparation:

1. Mix lemon juice, rosemary, thyme, oregano, salt, and coriander in a bowl.
2. Rub this mixture over the lamb chops and marinate for 10 minutes.
3. Place the lamb chops in the Ninja sheet pan.
4. Transfer the sheet pan to the Ninja Foodi Digital Air Fryer Oven and close the door.
5. Select "Air Roast" mode by rotating the dial.
6. Press the TEMP button and change the value to 390 degrees F.
7. Press the TIME button and change the value to 7 minutes, then press START to begin cooking.
8. Flip the chops once cooked halfway through, then resume cooking.
9. Serve warm.

Serving Suggestion: Serve the chops with fresh green and mashed potatoes.

Variation Tip: Add sweet potatoes or squash instead on the side of the chops before roasting.

Nutritional Information Per Serving:

Calories 301 | Fat 5g |Sodium 340mg | Carbs 24.7g | Fiber 1.2g | Sugar 1.3g | Protein 15.3g

Steak Bites Mushrooms

Prep Time: 15 minutes.

Cook Time: 15 minutes.

Serves: 2

Ingredients:

- 1 lb. steaks, cut into cubes
- 8 oz. mushrooms, halved
- 2 tablespoons butter, melted
- 1 teaspoon Worcestershire sauce
- ½ teaspoon garlic powder
- Salt, to taste
- Black pepper, to taste
- Chili flakes, for finishing

Preparation:

1. Toss steak cubes with mushrooms in a bowl.
2. Mix melted butter with garlic powder, black pepper, and Worcestershire sauce in a small bowl.
3. Spread the mushrooms and steak in the Ninja sheet pan.
4. Transfer the sheet pan to the Ninja Foodi Digital Air Fryer Oven and close the door.
5. Select "Air Roast" mode by rotating the dial.
6. Press the TEMP button and change the value to 400 degrees F.
7. Press the TIME button and change the value to 15 minutes, then press START to begin cooking.
8. Toss the steaks once cooked halfway through, then resume cooking.
9. Garnish with chili flakes, black pepper and salt.
10. Serve warm.

Serving Suggestion: Serve the steak and mushrooms with quinoa salad.

Variation Tip: Add barbecue sauce to the beef and mushrooms.

Nutritional Information Per Serving:

Calories 448 | Fat 23g |Sodium 350mg | Carbs 18g | Fiber 6.3g | Sugar 1g | Protein 40.3g

Glazed Steaks

Prep Time: 15 minutes.

Cook Time: 15 minutes.

Serves: 2

Ingredients:

- 2 (6 oz.) sirloin steaks
- 2 tablespoons soy sauce
- 1/2 tablespoons Worcestershire sauce
- 2 tablespoons brown sugar
- 1 tablespoon ginger, peeled and grated
- 1 tablespoon garlic, crushed
- 1 teaspoon seasoned salt
- Salt and black pepper, to taste

Preparation:

1. Mix soy sauce, Worcestershire sauce, brown sugar, ginger, salt and black pepper in a sealable bag.
2. Add steak to the spice blend and seal the bag.
3. Shake it well and marinate for 8 hours in the refrigerator.
4. Spread the steaks in the Ninja sheet pan.
5. Transfer the sheet pan to the Ninja Foodi Digital Air Fryer Oven and close the door.
6. Select "Air Roast" mode by rotating the dial.
7. Press the TEMP button and change the value to 400 degrees F.
8. Press the TIME button and change the value to 15 minutes, then press START to begin cooking.
9. Serve warm.

Serving Suggestion: Serve the beef steak with sautéed vegetables and toasted bread slices.

Variation Tip: Use honey instead of sugar for a mild sweet taste.

Nutritional Information Per Serving:

Calories 309 | Fat 25g |Sodium 463mg | Carbs 9.9g | Fiber 0.3g | Sugar 0.3g | Protein 18g

Bacon Meatloaf

Prep Time: 15 minutes.

Cook Time: 40 minutes.

Serves: 6

Ingredients:

- ½ lb. thick cut bacon
- ½ lb. ground beef
- ½ lb. ground pork
- 1 cup almond flour
- ½ yellow onion, diced
- 1 red bell pepper, diced
- 2 tablespoons ketchup
- 1 tablespoon spicy brown mustard
- 1 teaspoon salt

- 1 teaspoon garlic powder
- 1/2 teaspoon white pepper
- 1/2 teaspoon celery salt
- 1/4 teaspoon cayenne pepper
- 1 egg

Sauce:

- 1/2 cup ketchup
- 3 tablespoons maple syrup

Preparation:

1. Mix beef, pork, almond flour, and the rest of the meatloaf ingredients in a large bowl except bacon.
2. Spread the meatloaf mixture in a greased 9x5 inches meatloaf pan, then cover it with bacon slices.
3. Transfer the meatloaf pan to the Ninja Foodi Digital Air Fryer Oven and close the door.
4. Select "Air Roast" mode by rotating the dial.
5. Press the TEMP button and change the value to 350 degrees F.
6. Press the TIME button and change the value to 30 minutes, then press START to begin cooking.
7. Mix ketchup with maple syrup in a bowl.
8. Brush it with maple syrup and return it to the Ninja Digital Air Fryer oven.
9. Cook this meatloaf for another 10 minutes.
10. Slice and serve warm.

Serving Suggestion: Serve the meatloaf with mashed potatoes.

Variation Tip: Roast the meatloaf without bacon slices directly in a meatloaf pan.

Nutritional Information Per Serving:

Calories 537 | Fat 20g |Sodium 719mg | Carbs 25.1g | Fiber 0.9g | Sugar 1.4g | Protein 37.8g

Fish and Seafood

Sheet Pan Shrimp Asparagus Potato

Prep Time: 15 minutes.

Cook Time: 44 minutes.

Serves: 4

Ingredients:

- 1 lb. shrimp peeled, deveined
- 1 lb. baby potatoes, halved
- 1 lb. asparagus trimmed
- 16 cherry tomatoes
- 3 tablespoons olive oil
- 1/2 lemon, juiced
- 1 garlic clove, minced
- 1/2 teaspoon dried parsley
- 1/8 teaspoon crushed red pepper flakes
- Sea Salt, to taste
- Black Pepper, to taste

Preparation:

1. Toss potatoes with black pepper, salt and 1 tablespoon olive oil in the Ninja sheet pan.
2. Transfer the sheet pan to the Ninja Foodi Digital Air Fryer Oven and close the door.
3. Select "Air Roast" mode by rotating the dial.
4. Press the TEMP button and change the value to 400 degrees F.
5. Press the TIME button and change the value to 12 minutes, then press START to begin cooking.
6. Meanwhile, toss tomatoes with shrimp, lemon, garlic, parsley, crushed red pepper, sea salt and 1 tablespoon olive oil in a large bowl.
7. Push the roasted potatoes aside in the sheet pan and add asparagus and shrimp mixture.
8. Drizzle black pepper, salt and olive oil over the asparagus.
9. Transfer the sheet pan to the Ninja Foodi Digital Air Fryer Oven and close the door.
10. Press the TIME button and change the value to 10 minutes, then press START to begin cooking.
11. Once it's done, switch the Ninja digital Air Fryer oven to "Air broil" mode and cook for 2 minutes.
12. Serve warm.

Serving Suggestion: Serve the shrimp meal on top of the rice risotto.

Variation Tip: Add paprika for more spice.

Nutritional Information Per Serving:

Calories 448 | Fat 13g |Sodium 353mg | Carbs 31g | Fiber 0.4g | Sugar 1g | Protein 29g

Shrimp and Crab Casserole

Prep Time: 15 minutes.

Cook Time: 55 minutes.

Serves: 6

Ingredients:

- 2 (8 2/3 oz.) packages ready-to-serve long grain rice
- 1/4 cup butter, cubed
- 2 celery ribs, chopped
- 1 medium onion, chopped
- 3 tablespoons all-purpose flour
- 1 ½ cups half-and-half cream
- 3/4 teaspoon salt
- 1/2 teaspoon hot pepper sauce
- 1/4 teaspoon black pepper
- 1 teaspoon seafood seasoning
- 1 ½ lbs. shrimp, peeled and deveined
- 2 cans (6 oz.) lump crabmeat, drained
- 1 cup Colby-Monterey Jack cheese, shredded

Preparation:

1. Spread the long grain rice to a 13x9 inches baking dish.
2. Sauté celery and onion with butter in a skillet for 8 minutes.
3. Stir in flour and cream then mix well for 2 minutes.
4. Add black pepper, pepper sauce, salt and seafood seasoning.
5. Stir in shrimp, mix and spread this mixture over the rice.
6. Drizzle cheese on top and cover it a foil sheet.
7. Transfer the baking dish to the Ninja Foodi Digital Air Fryer Oven and close the door.
8. Select the "Bake" mode by rotating the dial.
9. Press the TEMP button and change the value to 350 degrees F.
10. Press the TIME button and change the value to 45 minutes, then press START to begin cooking.
11. Serve warm.

Serving Suggestion: Serve the casserole with crispy onion rings on the side.

Variation Tip: Add boiled pasta to the casserole and sliced jalapenos on top.

Nutritional Information Per Serving:

Calories 376 | Fat 17g |Sodium 1127mg | Carbs 24g | Fiber 1g | Sugar 3g | Protein 29g

Bacon Wrapped Shrimp

Prep Time: 15 minutes.

Cook Time: 10 minutes.

Serves: 6

Ingredients:

- 24 shrimp, deveined
- 8 bacon slices, cut into thirds
- 1 tablespoon olive oil
- 1 teaspoon paprika
- 2 garlic cloves, minced
- 1 tablespoon parsley, chopped

Preparation:

1. Mix parsley, garlic, paprika and olive oil in a large bowl.
2. Add shrimp then mix well to coat.
3. Wrap the bacon strips around each shrimp.
4. Place the wrapped shrimp, cover and refrigerate for 30 minutes.
5. Transfer the wrapped shrimp to the Air Fryer basket and spray them with cooking spray.
6. Transfer the sheet pan to the Ninja Foodi Digital Air Fryer Oven and close the door.
7. Select "Air Crisp" mode by rotating the dial.
8. Press the TEMP button and change the value to 400 degrees F.
9. Press the TIME button and change the value to 10 minutes, then press START to begin cooking.
10. Serve warm.

Serving Suggestion: Serve the shrimp with fresh greens and chili sauce on the side.

Variation Tip: Roll the wrapped shrimp in breadcrumbs for a crispy touch.

Nutritional Information Per Serving:

Calories 457 | Fat 19g |Sodium 557mg | Carbs 19g | Fiber 1.8g | Sugar 1.2g | Protein 32.5g

Lemon Shrimp and Vegetables

Prep Time: 15 minutes.

Cook Time: 6 minutes.

Serves: 4

Ingredients:

- 1 cup broccoli, chopped
- 1 cup cauliflower, chopped
- 12 oz. small shrimp
- 1 tablespoons garlic and herb seasoning
- 2 tablespoons olive oil
- Juice half lemon
- Salt and black pepper, to taste

Preparation:

1. Toss shrimp and veggies in a large bowl.
2. Add garlic seasoning, olive oil, lemon juice, black pepper and salt.
3. Mix well and spread the shrimp mixture on the Ninja baking sheet.
4. Transfer the basket to the Ninja Foodi Digital Air Fryer Oven and close the door.
5. Select "Air Crisp" mode by rotating the dial.
6. Press the TEMP button and change the value to 380 degrees F.
7. Press the TIME button and change the value to 6 minutes, then press START to begin cooking.
8. Toss the shrimp and veggies once cooked halfway through and resume cooking.
9. Serve warm.

Serving Suggestion: Serve the shrimp mix with alfredo sauce on top.

Variation Tip: Add zucchini noodles to the veggies and shrimp.

Nutritional Information Per Serving:

Calories 392 | Fat 16g |Sodium 466mg | Carbs 3.9g | Fiber 0.9g | Sugar 0.6g | Protein 48g

Mangalorean Fish Fry

Prep Time: 15 minutes.

Cook Time: 14 minutes.

Serves: 4

Ingredients:

- 1 teaspoon black peppercorns
- 1 teaspoon coriander seeds
- 1 teaspoon cumin seeds
- 1 teaspoon turmeric
- 1-inch piece of ginger
- 3 fresh garlic cloves, minced
- 15 curry leaves
- 1 tablespoon lime juice
- 2 lbs. salmon steaks
- 2 tablespoons coconut oil
- Extra lime juice

Preparation:

1. Roast coriander, black peppercorns, and cumin in a dry skillet for 4 minutes.
2. Transfer these spices to a grinder and grind them into a powder.
3. Add ginger, garlic, turmeric, and curry leaves, then blend until smooth.
4. Rub this paste over the fish, place it in a tray, and cover the fish for 30 minutes.
5. Place the fish in the Ninja Air Fryer basket and drizzle coconut oil.
6. Transfer the basket to the Ninja Foodi Digital Air Fryer Oven and close the door.
7. Select "Air Crisp" mode by rotating the dial.
8. Press the TEMP button and change the value to 400 degrees F.
9. Press the TIME button and change the value to 10 minutes, then press START to begin cooking.
10. Flip the fish once cooked halfway through and resume cooking.
11. Garnish with lime juice.
12. Serve warm.

Serving Suggestion: Serve the salmon fillets with fried rice.

Variation Tip: Air Fry the salmon with a lemon slice on top.

Nutritional Information Per Serving:

Calories 321 | Fat 7.4g |Sodium 356mg | Carbs 9.3g | Fiber 2.4g | Sugar 5g | Protein 37.2g

Garlic Parmesan Shrimp

Prep Time: 15 minutes.

Cook Time: 12 minutes.

Serves: 4

Ingredients:

- 1 lb. shrimp, peeled and deveined
- 2 tablespoons olive oil
- ⅛ teaspoons garlic powder
- ½ teaspoons salt
- ½ teaspoons black pepper
- 2 tablespoons parmesan cheese, grated
- 2 tablespoons parsley, minced

Preparation:

1. Mix parsley, cheese, black pepper, salt, garlic powder, and olive oil in a bowl.
2. Toss in shrimp, then mix well to coat.
3. Spread the shrimp in the Ninja sheet pan.
4. Transfer the sheet pan to the Ninja Foodi Digital Air Fryer Oven and close the door.
5. Select "Air Roast" mode by rotating the dial.
6. Press the TEMP button and change the value to 350 degrees F.
7. Press the TIME button and change the value to 12 minutes, then press START to begin cooking.
8. Serve warm.

Serving Suggestion: Serve the shrimp with vegetable rice.

Variation Tip: Add canned corn to the shrimp.

Nutritional Information Per Serving:

Calories 258 | Fat 9g |Sodium 994mg | Carbs 1g | Fiber 0.4g | Sugar 3g | Protein 16g

Baked Salmon

Prep Time: 15 minutes

Cook Time: 10 minutes.

Serves: 2

Ingredients:

- 2 (6 oz.) salmon fillets
- 1 teaspoon olive oil
- Salt, to taste
- Black pepper, to taste

Preparation:

1. Rub the salmon with olive oil, black pepper and salt.
2. Place the salmon in the Ninja Air Fryer basket.
3. Transfer the basket to the Ninja Foodi Digital Air Fryer Oven and close the door.
4. Select "Air Crisp" mode by rotating the dial.
5. Press the TEMP button and change the value to 360 degrees F.
6. Press the TIME button and change the value to 10 minutes, then press START to begin cooking.
7. Serve warm.

Serving Suggestion: Serve the salmon with lemon slices and fried rice.

Variation Tip: Use white pepper for a change of flavor.

Nutritional Information Per Serving:

Calories 378 | Fat 21g |Sodium 146mg | Carbs 7.1g | Fiber 0.1g | Sugar 0.4g | Protein 23g

Crusted Tilapia

Prep Time: 15 minutes.

Cook Time: 10 minutes.

Serves: 4

Ingredients:

- 4 Tilapia fillets
- 1/2 cup flour
- 4 oz. parmesan cheese, grated
- 2 teaspoons lemon zest
- 1 teaspoon salt
- 1 teaspoon garlic powder
- 1/2 teaspoon black pepper
- 1/2 teaspoon paprika
- 2 eggs

Preparation:

1. Spread flour in a bowl, beat eggs in another bowl and mix parmesan cheese with lemon zest, salt, black pepper, garlic powder and paprika in a shallow tray.
2. Coat the tilapia with flour, dip it in the eggs and coat with parmesan mixture.
3. Place the tilapia fillets in the Ninja sheet pan, lined with parchment paper.
4. Transfer the sheet pan to the Ninja Foodi Digital Air Fryer Oven and close the door.
5. Select "Air Roast" mode by rotating the dial.
6. Press the TEMP button and change the value to 400 degrees F.
7. Press the TIME button and change the value to 10 minutes, then press START to begin cooking.
8. Flip the fish once cooked halfway through and resume cooking.
9. Serve warm.

Serving Suggestion: Serve the tilapia with boiled eggs and fresh greens.

Variation Tip: Drizzle cheddar cheese on top for a rich taste.

Nutritional Information Per Serving:

Calories 351 | Fat 4g |Sodium 236mg | Carbs 19.1g | Fiber 0.3g | Sugar 0.1g | Protein 36g

Cajun Shrimp

Prep Time: 15 minutes.

Cook Time: 8 minutes.

Serves: 4

Ingredients:

- 1 tablespoon Cajun seasoning
- 24 (1 lb.) shrimp, cleaned and peeled
- 6 oz. cooked turkey sausage, sliced
- 1 medium zucchini, sliced
- 1 medium yellow squash, sliced
- 1 red bell pepper, seeded and diced
- 1/4 teaspoon salt
- 2 tablespoons olive oil

Preparation:

1. Toss shrimp with Cajun seasoning in a large bowl.
2. Mix bell peppers, zucchini squash and sausage with oil in a bowl.
3. Spread the shrimp and veggies to the Ninja sheet pan.
4. Transfer the sheet pan to the Ninja Foodi Digital Air Fryer Oven and close the door.
5. Select "Air Roast" mode by rotating the dial.
6. Press the TEMP button and change the value to 400 degrees F.
7. Press the TIME button and change the value to 8 minutes, then press START to begin cooking.
8. Serve warm.

Serving Suggestion: Serve the shrimp meal with mashed potatoes.

Variation Tip: Spread crispy nachos at the base of the sheet pan before adding veggies and seafood.

Nutritional Information Per Serving:

Calories 378 | Fat 7g |Sodium 316mg | Carbs 16.2g | Fiber 0.3g | Sugar 0.3g | Protein 26g

Lobster Tail

Prep Time: 15 minutes.

Cook Time: 6 minutes.

Serves: 4

Ingredients:

- 4 lobster tails
- 2 tablespoons butter, melted
- 1/2 teaspoon salt
- 1 teaspoon black pepper

Preparation:

1. Cut the lobster tails from the top to open the shell and place the tail in the Ninja Air Fryer basket.
2. Drizzle butter, black pepper, and salt on top.
3. Transfer the basket to the Ninja Foodi Digital Air Fryer Oven and close the door.
4. Select "Air Crisp" mode by rotating the dial.
5. Press the TEMP button and change the value to 380 degrees F.
6. Press the TIME button and change the value to 6 minutes, then press START to begin cooking.
7. Serve warm.

Serving Suggestion: Serve the lobster tail with roasted broccoli florets.

Variation Tip: Drizzle lemon garlic butter on top before cooking.

Nutritional Information Per Serving:

Calories 415 | Fat 15g |Sodium 634mg | Carbs 14.3g | Fiber 1.4g | Sugar 1g | Protein 23.3g

Crab Rangoon

Prep Time: 15 minutes.

Cook Time: 5 minutes.

Serves: 6

Ingredients:

- 2 oz. imitation crab meat
- 2 oz. cream cheese
- 1½ tablespoons green onions chopped
- ½ tablespoons Worcestershire sauce
- 16 wonton wrappers
- Cooking oil for spritzing

Preparation:

1. Mix crab meat with cream cheese, green onions, and Worcestershire sauce in a bowl.
2. Spread the wonton wrapper on the working surface.
3. Divide the crab filling at the center of each wrapper then wet its edges.
4. Bring the four corners of each wrapper and pinch the edges together.
5. Place the crab Rangoon in the Ninja Air Fryer basket and spray them with cooking spray.
6. Transfer the basket to the Ninja Foodi Digital Air Fryer Oven and close the door.
7. Select "Air Crisp" mode by rotating the dial.
8. Press the TEMP button and change the value to 350 degrees F.
9. Press the TIME button and change the value to 5 minutes, then press START to begin cooking.
10. Serve warm.

Serving Suggestion: Serve the Rangoon's with tomato ketchup.

Variation Tip: Add garlic salt to the filling for more taste.

Nutritional Information Per Serving:

Calories 251 | Fat 17g |Sodium 723mg | Carbs 21g | Fiber 2.5g | Sugar 2g | Protein 7.3g

Vegetables and Sides

Loaded Tater Tots

Prep Time: 15 minutes.
Cook Time: 25 minutes.
Serves: 4

Ingredients:

- 2 lbs. frozen tater tots
- 1/2 cup crumbled feta cheese
- 1/4 cup red onion, peeled, diced
- 1/4 cup black olives, sliced
- Fresh dill, for garnish

Tzatziki Sauce

- 1 cup Greek yogurt
- 1 English cucumber, grated
- 3 garlic cloves, peeled, minced
- 2 tablespoons fresh lemon juice

- 3 tablespoons fresh dill, chopped
- 1 teaspoon salt
- 1 teaspoon black pepper

Preparation:

1. Prepare the tzatziki sauce by mixing all the ingredients in a bowl.
2. Cover and refrigerate the sauce until the tater tots are ready.
3. Spread the tater tots in the Ninja Air Fryer basket.
4. Transfer the basket to the Ninja Foodi Digital Air Fryer Oven and close the door.
5. Select "Air Crisp" mode by rotating the dial.
6. Press the TEMP button and change the value to 450 degrees F.
7. Press the TIME button and change the value to 15 minutes, then press START to begin cooking.
8. Transfer the tater tots to the Ninja sheet pan.
9. Add feta cheese, olives, and red onion on top.
10. Return the sheet pan to the Ninja digital Air Fryer oven.
11. Select the "Bake" mode by rotating the dial.
12. Press the TEMP button and change the value to 350 degrees F.
13. Press the TIME button and change the value to 10 minutes, then press START to begin cooking.
14. Serve the tater tots with the tzatziki sauce.

Serving Suggestion: Serve the tater tots with guacamole on top.

Variation Tip: Add olives or sliced mushrooms.

Nutritional Information Per Serving:

Calories 246 | Fat 15g |Sodium 220mg | Carbs 40.3g | Fiber 2.4g | Sugar 1.2g | Protein 12.4g

Kale and Potato Nuggets

Prep Time: 15 minutes.

Cook Time: 45 minutes.

Serves: 6

Ingredients:

- 2 cups potatoes, chopped
- 1 teaspoon olive oil
- 1 garlic clove, minced
- 4 cups kale, chopped
- 1/8 cup almond milk
- 1/4 teaspoon sea salt
- 1/8 teaspoon black pepper
- Cooking oil spray

Preparation:

1. Boil potatoes in boiling water in a cooking pot for 30 minutes, then drain.
2. Sauté garlic with oil in a skillet for 1 minute.
3. Stir in kale and cook for 3 minutes, then transfer to a bowl.
4. Mash boiled potatoes in a medium bowl, then milk, black pepper, and salt.
5. Mix well, then add kale mixture and stir well.
6. Make 1-inch nuggets out of this mixture and place the nuggets in the Ninja Air Fryer basket, then coat them with cooking oil.
7. Transfer the basket to the Ninja Foodi Digital Air Fryer Oven and close the door.
8. Select "Air Crisp" mode by rotating the dial.
9. Press the TEMP button and change the value to 400 degrees F.
10. Press the TIME button and change the value to 12 minutes, then press START to begin cooking.
11. Toss the nuggets once cooked halfway through and resume cooking.
12. Serve warm.

Serving Suggestion: Serve the potato nuggets with pita bread and chili sauce.

Variation Tip: Add boiled and mashed chickpeas to the batter

Nutritional Information Per Serving:

Calories 338 | Fat 24g |Sodium 620mg | Carbs 58.3g | Fiber 2.4g | Sugar 1.2g | Protein 5.4g

Spicy Cauliflower Stir-Fry

Prep Time: 15 minutes.

Cook Time: 20 minutes.

Serves: 4

Ingredients:

- 1 head cauliflower, florets
- ¾ cup onion white, sliced
- 5 garlic cloves, sliced
- 1 ½ tablespoons tamari
- 1 tablespoon rice vinegar
- ½ teaspoon coconut sugar
- 1 tablespoon Sriracha
- 2 scallions for garnish

Preparation:

1. Spread the cauliflower in the Ninja Air Fryer basket.
2. Transfer the basket to the Ninja Foodi Digital Air Fryer Oven and close the door.
3. Select "Air Crisp" mode by rotating the dial.
4. Press the TEMP button and change the value to 350 degrees F.
5. Press the TIME button and change the value to 10 minutes, then press START to begin cooking.
6. Add sliced onion and garlic to the cauliflower to Air Frye for 5 minutes.
7. Meanwhile, mix black pepper, salt, sriracha, coconut sugar, and rice vinegar in a bowl.
8. Pour this mixture over the cauliflower and onion, then cook for 5 minutes.
9. Garnish with scallions.
10. Serve warm.

Serving Suggestion: Serve the cauliflower with lemon wedges.

Variation Tip: Add breadcrumbs to the florets before baking for a crispy texture.

Nutritional Information Per Serving:

Calories 93 | Fat 3g |Sodium 510mg | Carbs 12g | Fiber 3g | Sugar 4g | Protein 4g

Kale Salad with Roasted Veggies

Prep Time: 15 minutes.
Cook Time: 23 minutes.
Serves: 4

Ingredients:

- 6 tablespoons olive oil
- 2 tablespoons balsamic vinegar
- 1 tablespoon tamari
- 2 garlic cloves, smashed
- ½ teaspoon dried basil
- ½ teaspoon dried rosemary
- 1 tablespoons shallot, chopped
- Black pepper, to taste
- Juice of 1 lemon
- 10 oz. baby Bella mushrooms, quartered
- 1-pint grape tomatoes
- 2 medium zucchinis, diced
- 1 medium red onion, diced
- Salt, to taste
- 1 bunch green kale, roughly chopped
- ½ cup parmesan cheese, grated

Preparation:

1. Toss mushrooms with garlic, tamari, 1 tablespoon balsamic, 2 tablespoons olive oil, black pepper, lemon juice, and dried herbs in a bowl.
2. Cover and refrigerate the mixture for 30 minutes.
3. Meanwhile, mix zucchini, onion and tomatoes with 3 tablespoons in a bowl.
4. Spread the veggies and marinated mushrooms to the Ninja sheet pan.
5. Transfer the sheet pan to the Ninja Foodi Digital Air Fryer Oven and close the door.
6. Select the "Bake" mode by rotating the dial.
7. Press the TEMP button and change the value to 425 degrees F.
8. Press the TIME button and change the value to 20 minutes, then press START to begin cooking.
9. Toss the veggies once cooked halfway through and resume cooking.
10. Meanwhile, mix kale with salt in a bowl, then sauté with 1 tablespoon olive oil, lemon juice, and balsamic vinegar in a pan for 3 minutes.
11. Toss the veggies with kales in a salad bowl.
12. Drizzle parmesan cheese on top.
13. Serve.

Serving Suggestion: Serve the kale salad with mashed potatoes.

Variation Tip: Add boiled couscous to the salad.

Nutritional Information Per Serving:
Calories 378 | Fat 3.8g |Sodium 620mg | Carbs 13.3g | Fiber 2.4g | Sugar 1.2g | Protein 5.4g

Sheet Pan Tofu Dinner

Prep Time: 15 minutes.

Cook Time: 30 minutes.

Serves: 4

Ingredients:

- 1 (14-oz.) package tofu, cut into cubes
- 2 medium carrots, peeled and cut into chunks
- 1 small head cauliflower, florets
- 1 medium sweet potato, peeled and diced
- 1 small red onion, quartered
- 1 small bunch asparagus, trimmed
- 4 tablespoons olive oil
- Salt, to taste
- Black pepper, to taste

Preparation:

1. Season the tofu with black pepper, salt and oil in a bowl.
2. Mix carrots, cauliflower, sweet potato, red onion, olive oil, salt and black pepper in a bowl for seasoning
3. Spread tofu and veggies in the Ninja sheet pan.
4. Transfer the sheet pan to the Ninja Foodi Digital Air Fryer Oven and close the door.
5. Select "Air Roast" mode by rotating the dial.
6. Press the TEMP button and change the value to 425 degrees F.
7. Press the TIME button and change the value to 15 minutes, then press START to begin cooking.
8. Toss asparagus with olive oil, black pepper, and salt.
9. Add this asparagus to the Ninja sheet pan and return it to the Ninja digital Air Fryer oven.
10. Continue baking the veggies for 15 minutes.
11. Serve warm.

Serving Suggestion: Serve the tofu dinner with crispy nachos and mashed potatoes.

Variation Tip: Add crispy dried onion for better taste.

Nutritional Information Per Serving:
Calories 304 | Fat 31g |Sodium 834mg | Carbs 21.4g | Fiber 0.2g | Sugar 0.3g | Protein 4.6g

Eggplant Parmesan

Prep Time: 15 minutes.

Cook Time: 25 minutes.

Serves: 4

Ingredients:

- 2 eggs
- 1 tablespoon water
- 1 cup panko breadcrumbs
- 1/4 cup grated parmesan cheese
- 1 teaspoon dried oregano
- 1 teaspoon dried basil
- 1/2 teaspoon garlic powder
- 2 tablespoons olive oil

- 1 eggplant, cut into ¼ -inch thick slices
- 1 (25 oz.) jar marinara sauce
- 8 oz. mozzarella cheese, shredded
- julienned fresh basil,

Preparation:

1. Place the eggplant in a colander and drizzle salt on top. Leave it for 15 minutes to drain excess water.
2. Pat dry the eggplant slices and place them on a plate.
3. Mix panko breadcrumbs with dried oregano, garlic powder, dried basil, and parmesan cheese in a shallow tray.
4. Beat eggs with water in a shallow bowl.
5. First, dip the eggplant slices in the egg wash, then coat them with breadcrumbs mixture.
6. Place the eggplant slices in the Ninja sheet pan and drizzle olive oil on top.
7. Transfer the sheet pan to the Ninja Foodi Digital Air Fryer Oven and close the door.
8. Select the "Bake" mode by rotating the dial.
9. Press the TEMP button and change the value to 350 degrees F.
10. Press the TIME button and change the value to 15 minutes, then press START to begin cooking.
11. Flip the eggplant slices and drizzle mozzarella cheese on top.
12. Continue baking these slices for 10 minutes in the Ninja digital Air Fryer oven.
13. Serve warm.

Serving Suggestion: Serve the eggplant with spaghetti or any other pasta.

Variation Tip: Top the eggplant slice with a pepperoni slice before adding cheese and cooking.

Nutritional Information Per Serving:

Calories 341 | Fat 24g |Sodium 547mg | Carbs 36.4g | Fiber 1.2g | Sugar 1g | Protein 10.3g

Herbed Potato, Asparagus, and Chickpea

Prep Time: 15 minutes.

Cook Time: 35 minutes.

Serves: 4

Ingredients:

- 1 lb. baby potatoes, sliced
- 1 ½ cups baby carrots
- 1 can (14oz.) chickpeas, drained and rinsed
- 1 teaspoon dried basil
- 1 teaspoon dried thyme
- 1 teaspoon dried oregano
- 1 teaspoon paprika
- ½ teaspoon garlic powder
- 3 tablespoons olive oil

- 1 lb. asparagus, trimmed and cut into thirds
- ½ large yellow onion, sliced
- Salt and black pepper, to taste
- Fresh parsley, to serve

Preparation:

1. Toss chickpeas, carrots, and potatoes with 1 ½ tablespoon oil and ¾ spices in a large bowl.
2. Spread the mixture in the Ninja sheet pan.
3. Transfer the sheet pan to the Ninja Foodi Digital Air Fryer Oven and close the door.
4. Select "Air Roast" mode by rotating the dial.
5. Press the TEMP button and change the value to 425 degrees F.
6. Press the TIME button and change the value to 25 minutes, then press START to begin cooking.
7. Toss asparagus and onion with rest of the ingredients in a tray.
8. Add these veggies to the sheet pan and return it to the Ninja digital Air Fryer oven.
9. Cook for another 15 minutes.
10. Serve warm.

Serving Suggestion: Serve the veggies with white rice or spaghetti squash.

Variation Tip: Add green beans instead of asparagus.

Nutritional Information Per Serving:

Calories 318 | Fat 15.7g |Sodium 124mg | Carbs 27g | Fiber 0.1g | Sugar 0.3g | Protein 4.9g

Sheet Pan Fajitas

Prep Time: 15 minutes.

Cook Time: 15 minutes.

Serves: 6

Ingredients:

- 3 bell peppers, sliced
- 1 large yellow onion, sliced
- 1 (15oz.) can pinto beans, drained, rinsed
- 1 tablespoon olive oil
- 1/4 teaspoon paprika
- 1/4 teaspoon garlic powder
- 1/4 teaspoon cumin
- 1/4 teaspoon salt
- 1/4 cup cheddar cheese, shredded
- Tortillas for serving

Preparation:

1. Spread the pinto beans in the Ninja Sheet pan, lined with parchment paper.
2. Top the beans with bell peppers, yellow onion, olive oil, paprika, garlic powder, cumin, salt, and cheese
3. Transfer the sheet pan to the Ninja Foodi Digital Air Fryer Oven and close the door.
4. Select the "Bake" mode by rotating the dial.
5. Press the TEMP button and change the value to 350 degrees F.
6. Press the TIME button and change the value to 15 minutes, then press START to begin cooking.
7. Serve in tortillas.

Serving Suggestion: Serve the nachos with tomato sauce or guacamole.

Variation Tip: Add crushed tomatoes for a saucy texture.

Nutritional Information Per Serving:

Calories 391 | Fat 2.2g |Sodium 276mg | Carbs 27.7g | Fiber 0.9g | Sugar 1.4g | Protein 8.8g

Tofu Butternut Squash Dinner

Prep Time: 15 minutes.

Cook Time: 20 minutes.

Serves: 6

Ingredients:

- 1 package sprouted tofu, diced
- 12 oz. frozen butternut squash. cubed
- 12 oz. frozen pearl onions
- 1 red bell pepper, cut into chunks
- 3 frozen garlic cubes
- 12 oz. frozen broccoli florets

Preparation:

1. Toss tofu, butternut cubes, pearl onions, red bell pepper, garlic cubes, and broccoli florets in a bowl.
2. Spread the veggies and tofu in the Ninja sheet pan.
3. Transfer the sheet pan to the Ninja Foodi Digital Air Fryer Oven and close the door.
4. Select the "Bake" mode by rotating the dial.
5. Press the TEMP button and change the value to 400 degrees F.
6. Press the TIME button and change the value to 20 minutes, then press START to begin cooking.
7. Serve warm.

Serving Suggestion: Serve the tofu with roasted mushrooms.

Variation Tip: Add lemon zest and lemon juice for better taste.

Nutritional Information Per Serving:

Calories 324 | Fat 5g |Sodium 432mg | Carbs 13.1g | Fiber 0.3g | Sugar 1g | Protein 5.7g

Artichoke Spinach Casserole

Prep Time: 15 minutes.

Cook Time: 35 minutes.

Serves: 8

Ingredients:

- 1 lb. mushrooms, sliced
- 1/3 cup chicken broth
- 1 tablespoon all-purpose flour
- ½ cup evaporated milk
- 4 (10 oz.) packages spinach, thawed
- 2 cans (14 oz.) artichoke hearts, drained and sliced
- 1 cup sour cream
- ½ cup mayonnaise
- 3 tablespoons lemon juice
- ½ teaspoon garlic powder
- ¼ teaspoon salt
- 2 cans (14 ½ oz.) tomatoes, diced and drained
- ¼ teaspoon black pepper
- Paprika, for topping

Preparation:

1. Cook mushrooms with broth in a cooking pot for 3 minutes. Transfer the mushrooms to a plate using a slotted spoon.
2. Mix flour with milk in a bowl until smooth.
3. Pour this mixture into the broth and cook for 2 minutes until the mixture thickens.
4. Add tomatoes, mushrooms and spinach to the sauce.
5. Spread the artichoke hearts in a 13x9 inches casserole dish.
6. Add the spinach mixture on top.
7. Whisk sour cream with lemon juice, mayonnaise, salt, black pepper and garlic powder in a bowl.
8. Spread this mayo mixture on top and drizzle paprika on top.
9. Transfer the casserole dish to the Ninja Foodi Digital Air Fryer Oven and close the door.
10. Select the "Bake" mode by rotating the dial.
11. Press the TEMP button and change the value to 350 degrees F.
12. Press the TIME button and change the value to 30 minutes, then press START to begin cooking.
13. Serve warm.

Serving Suggestion: Serve the casserole with sautéed asparagus and toasted bread slices.

Variation Tip: Add boiled pasta to the casserole.

Nutritional Information Per Serving:

Calories 136 | Fat 10g |Sodium 249mg | Carbs 8g | Fiber 2g | Sugar 3g | Protein 4g

Porcini Mac and Cheese

Prep Time: 15 minutes.

Cook Time: 60 minutes.

Serves: 8

Ingredients:

- 1 (1 oz.) package dried porcini mushrooms
- 1 cup boiling water
- 1 (16 oz.) package pasta shells
- 6 tablespoons butter, cubed
- 1 cup baby portobello mushrooms, chopped
- 1 shallot, chopped
- 1 garlic clove, minced
- 3 tablespoons all-purpose flour
- 2 ½ cups milk
- 1/2 cup pumpkin ale
- 2 cups cheddar cheese, shredded
- 1 cup shredded fontina cheese
- 1 teaspoon salt
- 1 cup bread crumbs

Preparation:

1. Soak dried mushroom in boiling water for 20 minutes, then drain.
2. Boil pasta as per the cooking instructions and drain.
3. Sauté portobello mushrooms with butter and shallot in a Dutch oven for 3 minutes.
4. Stir in garlic then sauté for 1 minute then add flour, beer and milk.
5. Mix and cook for 4 minutes until the mixture thickens.
6. Stir in cheese, salt, dried mushrooms and mix well then spread the mixture in a 13x9inches casserole dish.
7. Transfer the casserole dish to the Ninja Foodi Digital Air Fryer Oven and close the door.
8. Select the "Bake" mode by rotating the dial.
9. Press the TEMP button and change the value to 350 degrees F.
10. Press the TIME button and change the value to 35 minutes, then press START to begin cooking.
11. Serve warm.

Serving Suggestion: Serve the mac and cheese with roasted veggies on the side.

Variation Tip: Add canned corn to the casserole.

Nutritional Information Per Serving:

Calories 351 | Fat 19g |Sodium 412mg | Carbs 43g | Fiber 0.3g | Sugar 1g | Protein 23g

Dessert Recipes

French Toast Sticks with Berries

Prep Time: 15 minutes.

Cook Time: 10 minutes.

Serves: 4

Ingredients:

- 4 (1 ½ oz.) whole-grain bread slices
- 2 large eggs
- 1/4 cup milk
- 1 teaspoon vanilla extract
- 1/2 teaspoon ground cinnamon
- 1/4 cup packed light brown sugar
- 2/3 cup flax seed meal
- Cooking spray

- 2 cups sliced fresh strawberries
- 8 teaspoons pure maple syrup
- 1 teaspoon powdered sugar

Preparation:

1. Cut the bread slices into 4 sticks and keep them aside.
2. Beat eggs with 1 tablespoon sugar, cinnamon, vanilla, and milk in a bowl.
3. Whisk flaxseed with 3 tablespoons sugar in a shallow tray.
4. Dip each breadstick in the egg mixture and coat them with a flaxseed mixture.
5. Place the coated breadsticks in the Ninja baking tray.
6. Transfer the basket to the Ninja Foodi Digital Air Fryer Oven and close the door.
7. Select "Air Crisp" mode by rotating the dial.
8. Press the TEMP button and change the value to 375 degrees F.
9. Press the TIME button and change the value to 10 minutes, then press START to begin cooking.
10. Flip the bread once cooked halfway through, then resume cooking.
11. Toss strawberries with maple syrup and sugar in a bowl.
12. Serve the French sticks with strawberry mixture.
13. Enjoy.

Serving Suggestion: Serve the bread slices with chocolate dip.

Variation Tip: Skip the flaxseed meal if not available and directly cook the French toasts after egg-milk coating.

Nutritional Information Per Serving:

Calories 361 | Fat 10g |Sodium 218mg | Carbs 56g | Fiber 10g | Sugar 30g | Protein 14g

Strawberry Roll Cake

Prep Time: 15 minutes.

Cook Time: 12 minutes.

Serves: 8

Ingredients:

Sponge Cake

- ½ cup sugar
- 4 large eggs
- ¾ cup all-purpose flour

- 1 teaspoon vanilla extract

Filling:

- ½ cup heavy whipping cream
- 1 cup butter salted
- 1 cup confectioner sugar

- 2 teaspoons vanilla extract
- 8 oz. strawberry preserves

Preparation:

1. Beat eggs with sugar in the bowl of a stand mixer until fluffy and pale.
2. Stir in all-purpose flour and vanilla extract, then mix well for 5 minutes until smooth.
3. Grease a 13x13 inch baking pan with butter and layer it with parchment paper.
4. Spread the batter in the baking pan.
5. Transfer the baking pan to the Ninja Foodi Digital Air Fryer Oven and close the door.
6. Select the "Bake" mode by rotating the dial.
7. Press the TEMP button and change the value to 325 degrees F.
8. Press the TIME button and change the value to 12 minutes, then press START to begin cooking.
9. Allow the sponge cake to cool, then transfer to a working surface.
10. Beat cream, butter, vanilla, and sugar in a mixer until fluffy.
11. Spread a layer of prepared buttercream on top of the cake and top it with strawberry preserves.
12. Roll the cake and slice it into 2-inch-thick slices.
13. Serve.

Serving Suggestion: Serve the sponge cake roll with fresh berries on top.

Variation Tip: Add blueberry preserves to the fillings.

Nutritional Information Per Serving:

Calories 118 | Fat 20g |Sodium 192mg | Carbs 23.7g | Fiber 0.9g | Sugar 19g | Protein 5.2g-

Fudgy Brownies

Prep Time: 15 minutes.

Cook Time: 35 minutes.

Serves: 8

Ingredients:

- ¾ cup butter salted
- 1¾ cup dark chocolate chips
- 1 teaspoon espresso powder
- ¾ teaspoons sea salt
- 1½ cups sugar
- 5 large eggs
- ⅓ cup cooking oil
- 2 teaspoons vanilla extract
- ½ cup of cocoa powder
- 1½ cups all-purpose flour

Preparation:

1. Blend eggs, oil, sugar, and butter in a stand mixer for 3 minutes.
2. Melt 1 cup chocolate chips in a bowl by heating in the microwave.
3. Add the melted chocolate, flour, espresso powder, cocoa powder, and vanilla.
4. Mix well until it makes a batter, then fold in the remaining chocolate chips.
5. Spread the batter in an 11 ½ x 9 inches baking pan, lined with parchment paper.
6. Transfer the baking dish to the Ninja Foodi Digital Air Fryer Oven and close the door.
7. Select the "Bake" mode by rotating the dial.
8. Press the TEMP button and change the value to 325 degrees F.
9. Press the TIME button and change the value to 35 minutes, then press START to begin cooking.
10. Once done, remove the fudge from the pan and allow it to cool.
11. Slice and serve.

Serving Suggestion: Serve the fudge brownie with a scoop of vanilla cream on top.

Variation Tip: Add chopped nuts to the batter.

Nutritional Information Per Serving:
Calories 248 | Fat 16g |Sodium 95mg | Carbs 38.4g | Fiber 0.3g | Sugar 10g | Protein 14.1g

Glazed Donut

Prep Time: 15 minutes.
Cook Time: 15 minutes.
Serves: 10

Ingredients:

- 1 cup warm milk
- 2-1/2 teaspoons active dry yeast
- 1/4 cup 1 teaspoon granulated sugar
- 1/2 teaspoon salt
- 1 whole egg
- 1/4 cup unsalted butter, melted
- 3 cups all-purpose flour
- Cooking oil spray

Glaze

- 3 tablespoons unsalted butter
- 1 cup powdered sugar
- 1 teaspoon pure vanilla extract
- 2 tablespoons boiled water

Preparation:

1. Mix yeast with warm milk in a large bowl and leave it for 10 minutes.
2. Stir in sugar, salt, butter, and egg, then beat until sugar is dissolved.
3. Add flour, then mix until it makes a smooth dough.
4. Knead this dough for 5 minutes, place it in a greased bowl then cover with a plastic wrap.
5. Leave the dough for 1 hour, then punch it down.
6. Roll the dough into a ½ inch thick sheet and cut the 12 donuts out of this dough.
7. Place the donuts in a Ninja sheet pan lined with parchment paper.
8. Cover the donuts with a kitchen towel and leave them for 30 minutes.
9. Brush the top of the donuts with cooking oil.
10. Transfer the sheet pan to the Ninja Foodi Digital Air Fryer Oven and close the door.
11. Select the "Bake" mode by rotating the dial.
12. Press the TEMP button and change the value to 350 degrees F.
13. Press the TIME button and change the value to 10 minutes, then press START to begin cooking.
14. Meanwhile, mix the ingredients donut glaze ingredients in a saucepan.
15. Stir and cook for 5 minutes, then allow it to cool.
16. Brush the baked donuts with this glaze and leave them for 10 minutes.
17. Serve.

Serving Suggestion: Serve the donuts with chocolate or apple sauce.

Variation Tip: Dip the donuts in chocolate syrup.

Nutritional Information Per Serving:
Calories 117 | Fat 12g |Sodium 79mg | Carbs 24.8g | Fiber 1.1g | Sugar 18g | Protein 5g

Carrot Cake

Prep Time: 15 minutes.

Cook Time: 30 minutes.

Serves: 8

Ingredients:

- 5 oz. brown sugar
- 2 eggs, beaten
- 5 oz. butter
- 1 orange, zest, and juice
- 7 oz. self-rising flour
- 1 teaspoon ground cinnamon
- 2 medium carrots, grated
- 20 oz. sultanas

Preparation:

1. Beat eggs in a mixing bowl and stir in sugar, and butter then beat until sugar is dissolved.
2. Stir in flour and mix until it makes a smooth batter.
3. Fold in sultanas, grated carrots, orange juice, and orange zest.
4. Mix well, then spread this batter in a greased baking dish.
5. Transfer the baking dish to the Ninja Foodi Digital Air Fryer Oven and close the door.
6. Select the "Bake" mode by rotating the dial.
7. Press the TEMP button and change the value to 350 degrees F.
8. Press the TIME button and change the value to 30 minutes, then press START to begin cooking.
9. Once done, allow the cake to cool.
10. Slice and serve.

Serving Suggestion: Serve the cake with creamy frosting on top.

Variation Tip: Add chopped pecans or walnuts to the batter.

Nutritional Information Per Serving:

Calories 195 | Fat 3g |Sodium 355mg | Carbs 20g | Fiber 1g | Sugar 25g | Protein 1g

Bread Pudding

Prep Time: 15 minutes.

Cook Time: 15 minutes.

Serves: 6

Ingredients:

- 2 cups bread, cubed
- 1 egg
- 2/3 cup heavy cream
- 1/2 teaspoon vanilla extract
- 1/4 cup sugar
- 1/4 cup chocolate chips

Preparation:

1. Beat egg with sugar, vanilla, and cream in a bowl.
2. Spread bread cubes and chocolate chips in the Ninja baking dish.
3. Pour the egg-sugar mixture over the bread cubes.
4. Transfer the baking dish to the Ninja Foodi Digital Air Fryer Oven and close the door.
5. Select the "Bake" mode by rotating the dial.
6. Press the TEMP button and change the value to 350 degrees F.
7. Press the TIME button and change the value to 15 minutes, then press START to begin cooking.
8. Allow the pudding to cool, then slice.
9. Serve.

Serving Suggestion: Serve the pudding with chocolate syrup on top.

Variation Tip: Add dried raisins instead of chocolate chips.

Nutritional Information Per Serving:

Calories 203 | Fat 8.9g |Sodium 340mg | Carbs 24.7g | Fiber 1.2g | Sugar 11.3g | Protein 5.3g

Sweet Apples

Prep Time: 15 minutes.

Cook Time: 9 minutes.

Serves: 6

Ingredients:

- 6 apples, cored and diced
- ¼ cup brown sugar
- ¼ cup white sugar
- ¼ teaspoon ground cloves
- ¼ teaspoon pumpkin pie spice
- ½ teaspoon ground cinnamon
- ⅓ cup of water

Preparation:

1. Mix water with cloves, pie spice, cinnamon, white sugar, and brown sugar in a saucepan.
2. Cook this sugar mixture for 2 minutes until it thickens.
3. Toss in apples, mix well to coat then spread them in the Ninja Air Fryer basket.
4. Transfer the basket to the Ninja Foodi Digital Air Fryer Oven and close the door.
5. Select "Air Crips" mode by rotating the dial.
6. Press the TEMP button and change the value to 350 degrees F.
7. Press the TIME button and change the value to 6 minutes, then press START to begin cooking.
8. Allow the apples to cool then serve.

Serving Suggestion: Serve the apples with sweet cream cheese dip.

Variation Tip: Use apple sauce to season the apples.

Nutritional Information Per Serving:

Calories 153 | Fat 1g |Sodium 8mg | Carbs 66g | Fiber 0.8g | Sugar 56g | Protein 1g

Cinnamon Rolls

Prep Time: 15 minutes.

Cook Time: 9 minutes.

Serves: 8

Ingredients:

- 1 lb. bread dough, thawed
- ¼ cup butter, melted
- ¾ cup brown sugar
- 1½ tablespoons cinnamon ground

Cream cheese glaze

- 4 oz. cream cheese softened
- 2 tablespoons butter, softened
- 1¼ cups powdered sugar
- ½ teaspoon vanilla

Preparation:

1. Roll the bread dough on a floured surface into a 13x11 inches rectangle.
2. Brush its top with melted butter and drizzle cinnamon and sugar on top.
3. Roll the rectangle and slice the roll into 1-inch slices.
4. Place the roll in the Ninja sheet pan, greased with cooking oil.
5. Transfer the sheet to the Ninja Foodi Digital Air Fryer Oven and close the door.
6. Select the "Bake" mode by rotating the dial.
7. Press the TEMP button and change the value to 350 degrees F.
8. Press the TIME button and change the value to 9 minutes, then press START to begin cooking.
9. Beat cream cheese with butter, sugar, and vanilla in a bowl.
10. Serve the cinnamon rolls with cream cheese mixture on top.
11. Enjoy.

Serving Suggestion: Serve the cinnamon rolls with chocolate syrup on top.

Variation Tip: Add crushed walnuts or pecans to the filling.

Nutritional Information Per Serving:

Calories 198 | Fat 14g |Sodium 272mg | Carbs 34g | Fiber 1g | Sugar 9.3g | Protein 1.3g

Crispy Oreos

Prep Time: 15 minutes.

Cook Time: 8 minutes.

Serves: 8

Ingredients:

- 1 can crescents dough
- 8 Oreo cookies
- 2 tablespoons sugar

Preparation:

1. Spread the crescents dough on the working surface.
2. Cut the dough into 8 rounds and place the one cookie into each round.
3. Wrap the dough around the cookies and place them in the Ninja Air Fryer basket.
4. Transfer the cookies to the Ninja Foodi Digital Air Fryer Oven and close the door.
5. Select "Air Crisp" mode by rotating the dial.
6. Press the TEMP button and change the value to 350 degrees F.
7. Press the TIME button and change the value to 8 minutes, then press START to begin cooking.
8. Flip the cookies once cooked halfway through, then resume cooking.
9. Allow the cookies to cool then garnish with sugar.
10. Serve.

Serving Suggestion: Serve the Oreos with chocolate sauce.

Variation Tip: Roll the dough wrapped Oreos in crushed nuts or coconut flakes before cooking.

Nutritional Information Per Serving:

Calories 159 | Fat 3g |Sodium 277mg | Carbs 21g | Fiber 1g | Sugar 9g | Protein 2g

Molten Lava Cake

Prep Time: 15 minutes.

Cook Time: 12 minutes.

Serves: 6

Ingredients:

- 8 oz. chocolate, shredded
- 10 tablespoons butter
- 3 large eggs
- 3 egg yolks
- 1/2 teaspoon salt
- 1 1/2 cups powdered sugar
- 1/2 cup all-purpose flour

Preparation:

1. Grease six- 6 oz. ramekins with cooking spray.
2. Melt chocolate and butter in a glass bowl by heating in the microwave for 2 minutes.
3. Stir in flour, sugar and salt then mix well until it makes a smooth dough.
4. Stir in egg yolks and eggs then mix well.
5. Divide this batter in the ramekins and place them in the sheet pan.
Transfer the sheet pan to the Ninja Foodi Digital Air Fryer Oven and close the door.
6. Select the "Bake" mode by rotating the dial.
7. Press the TEMP button and change the value to 400 degrees F.
8. Press the TIME button and change the value to 10 minutes, then press START to begin cooking.
9. Allow the ramekins to cool then garnish with berries, sugar, and cream.
10. Serve.

Serving Suggestion: Serve the cakes with cream frosting on top.

Variation Tip: Add chocolate chips or a tsp of crushed nuts to the batter for the change of flavor.

Nutritional Information Per Serving:
Calories 245 | Fat 14g |Sodium 122mg | Carbs 23.3g | Fiber 1.2g | Sugar 12g | Protein 4.3g

3 Weeks Meal Plan:

Week 1

Day 1:

Breakfast: Ham Brie Sandwich

Lunch: Italian Turkey Breast

Snack: Sweet Potato Fries

Dinner: Lobster Tail

Dessert: Molten Lava Cake

Day 2:

Breakfast: Breakfast Hash

Lunch: Thanksgiving Turkey Meal

Snack: Corn on the Cob

Dinner: Garlic Parmesan Shrimp

Dessert: Crispy Oreos

Day 3:

Breakfast: Breakfast Frittata

Lunch: Turkey Meatloaf

Snack: Calzones

Dinner: Cajun Shrimp

Dessert: Cinnamon Rolls

Day 4:

Breakfast: Chile-Cheese Frittata

Lunch: General Tso's Chicken

Snack: Pita Pizzas

Dinner: Mangalorean Fish Fry

Dessert: Sweet Apples

Day 5:

Breakfast: Hasselback Potatoes

Snack: Spanakopita Bites

Lunch: Chicken Enchiladas

Dinner: Lemon Shrimp and Vegetables

Dessert: Bread Pudding

Day 6:

Breakfast: Morning Bagels

Lunch: Korean Chicken Wings

Snack: Pork Dumplings

Dinner: Shrimp and Crab Casserole

Dessert: Carrot Cake

Day 7:

Breakfast: Egg Avocado Boats

Lunch: Cheesy Chicken Nachos

Snack: Curry Chickpeas

Dinner: Crusted Tilapia

Dessert: Glazed Donut

Week 2

Day 1:

Breakfast: Ham Brie Sandwich

Lunch: Bacon Wrapped Shrimp

Snack: Sweet Potato Fries

Dinner: Italian Pasta Bake

Dessert: Molten Lava Cake

Day 2:

Breakfast: Breakfast Hash

Lunch: Sheet Pan Tofu Dinner

Snack: Turkey Croquettes

Dinner: Sausage Casserole

Dessert: Crispy Oreos

Day 3:

Breakfast: Breakfast Frittata

Lunch: Eggplant Parmesan

Snack: Pork Meatballs

Dinner: Christmas Casserole

Dessert: Cinnamon Rolls

Day 4:

Breakfast: Chile-Cheese Frittata

Lunch: Herbed Potato, Asparagus, and Chickpea

Snack: Crab Rangoon

Dinner: Bacon Meatloaf

Dessert: Sweet Apples

Day 5:

Breakfast: Hasselback Potatoes

Lunch: Porcini Mac and Cheese

Snack: Spanakopita Bites

Dinner: Steak Bites Mushrooms

Dessert: Bread Pudding

Day 6:

Breakfast: Morning Bagels

Lunch: Spicy Cauliflower Stir-Fry

Snack: Pork Dumplings

Dinner: Glazed Steaks

Dessert: Carrot Cake

Day 7:

Breakfast: Egg Avocado Boats

Lunch: Sheet Pan Fajitas

Snack: Kale Salad with Roasted Veggies

Dinner: Herbed Lamb Chops

Dessert: Glazed Donut

Week 3

Day 1:

Breakfast: Breakfast Bombs

Lunch: Artichoke Spinach Casserole

Snack: Kale and Potato Nuggets

Dinner: Lamb Chops with Garlic Sauce

Dessert: French Toast Sticks with Berries

Day 2:

Breakfast: Egg Avocado Boats

Lunch: Chicken, Sweet Potatoes and Broccoli

Snack: Cinnamon Apple Chips

Dinner: Lamb Sirloin Steak

Dessert: Fudgy Brownies

Day 3:

Breakfast: Chile-Cheese Frittata

Lunch: Chicken Sheet Pan Meal

Snack: Corn Dog Bites

Dinner: Tofu Butternut Squash Dinner

Dessert: Strawberry Roll Cake

Day 4:

Breakfast: Chile-Cheese Frittata

Lunch: General Tso's Chicken

Snack: Pita Pizzas

Dinner: Masala Chops

Dessert: Sweet Apples

Day 5:

Breakfast: Hasselback Potatoes

Lunch: Chicken Enchiladas

Snack: Spanakopita Bites

Dinner: Sheet Pan Pork with Apples

Dessert: Bread Pudding

Day 6:

Breakfast: Morning Bagels

Lunch: Korean Chicken Wings

Snack: Pork Dumplings

Dinner: Cauliflower pork casserole

Dessert: Carrot Cake

Day 7:

Breakfast: Egg Avocado Boats

Lunch: Cheesy Chicken Nachos

Snack: Curry Chickpeas

Dinner: Holiday Ham

Dessert: Glazed Donut

Conclusion

The Ninja Foodi Digital Air Fry Oven gives you a whole new experience of convenient cooking by bringing a variety of cooking styles into a single appliance. Where the Ninja foodi guarantees effective cooking with minimal supervision, this cookbook ensures that you get the most out of your Ninja Foodi Air Fry oven by developing its better understanding and by trying all sorts of recipes, including breakfasts, poultry, meat, snacks, seafood, and desserts, which are all shared in different chapters of this cookbook. With its single read, all the Ninja Foodi Air Fry oven beginners can readily learn basic techniques to bake and cook like a pro.

Remember, when you are done cooking with this digital oven, make sure to clean it thoroughly before putting it away. Thankfully the cleaning is quite when it comes to the Ninja Air Fryer ovens, especially when it comes to SP101 because due to its flip design, you can easily make it stand and open the lower power to remove the crumb tray and clean the oven inside out. After every session, the screen will show the "Red" hot sign on the screen until it is cooled. The moment it is cooled down, the screen shows a "Flip" sign, and the Hot sign disappears. Unplug the device carefully to cut off the power supply. Now remove all the removable items from inside the oven that may include the sheet pan, the wire rack, the Air Fryer basket, and crumb tray. Wash these removable items in the dishwasher or using the soapy water. Let them dry to use again. Hold the handle under the lid and flip the oven by pushing its front upward. Pull the base of the oven, and it will come out like the lid. Wipe off the base with the help of a wet cloth. Allow its base to dry out completely, then close it.

So, if you really want to avail all the smart cooking feature offered by this amazing cooking appliance, then it's about time that you adorn your kitchen counter with this smartly designed multipurpose oven, and then start cooking some magic at home using our special Ninja digital Air Fry oven recipe collection.

Made in the USA
Monee, IL
09 December 2020